GANNET

FROM THE COCKPIT, No 7

SIMON ASKINS

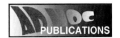

PUBLICATIONS

Contents

INTRODUCTION

Commander Simon Askins

BY the end of World War II, the well-proven method of submarine detection was either by aircraft radar, to find a submarine near or on the surface, by or ship's sonar, if the quarry was submerged. The destruction of the target was achieved by the aircraft dropping depth charges (if it arrived in time to attack) or, more usually, by a surface vessel using its sonar for pinpoint positioning and then attacking with depth charges or an ahead-throwing weapon such as 'Squid' or 'Hedgehog'.

In the immediate aftermath of the war, the Fleet Air Arm was developing its expertise in detecting submarines on the surface using the radar fitted in Swordfish and Firefly aircraft—and working with the frigates and destroyers to sink them. The logical next step was a 'combined' solution wherein one aircraft, or perhaps two working together, would be able to detect and attack a submarine. However, no aircraft then flying could fulfil this requirement. The Firefly, while quite good, was a modified attack aircraft which had fair speed and reasonable endurance; but what was now required was an aircraft with a high endurance for prolonged searches (hence good fuel consumption) yet having also a good cruising speed to arrive at the search area quickly, and equipped both with its own radar and sonar in order to locate a submarine and with the weapons necessary to destroy it.

A Fairey Gannet A.E.W. Mk 3 of 849 Squadron about to engage a wire on board HMS *Ark Royal*, June 1974.

To fulfil this requirement, the Fairey Aviation Company produced the Gannet, of which there were, finally, six different marks (arising from changing requirements and tasks). The development and production of the A.E.W. Mk 3 in the late 1950s overlapped with the government decision to rationalise aircraft production with fewer manufacturers. Fairey was instructed to move out of airframe design when the Ministry of Defence completed a major review of how it saw the future of warfare—which did not include manned aircraft! Fairey therefore handed the design authority for the Gannet to Westland Aircraft at Yeovil, Somerset. Naturally, most of the design team went with it, although the Hayes factory continued producing aircraft as it had done for a number of years. The final batch of Mk 3 Gannets was built at Hayes in 1963 and test flown from White Waltham airfield.

The Gannet was the last in a long line of fixed-wing aircraft produced by Fairey. These had served the Fleet Air Arm well, and with distinction, since World War I—from the Fairey Hamble Baby seaplane of 1917 (and its land equivalent used at RNAS Cranwell) through the World War II Swordfish, Fulmar, Barracuda and Firefly (the last-named serving also in Korean War). In fact, the only later complete aircraft produced by Fairey after the Gannet were the Delta 2 supersonic research aircraft (in 1956) and the Rotodyne (which first flew in 1957). Thereafter, Fairey became Fairey Hydraulics Ltd, concentrating on components of that nature only.

COURTESY PHILIP JARRETT

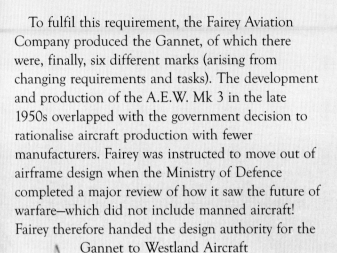

REQUIREMENT

Commander Simon Askins

IN 1946 the Admiralty decided to take a step forward and issued Operational Requirement OR.220 to build two anti-submarine aircraft to Specification GR.17/45. The aircraft, with two crew, would replace the Firefly but carry its own radar and the means of prosecuting the destruction of any submarine found. The Firefly had been limited by its lack of capacity for disposable weight (in the form of fuel and weapons), and the new requirement demanded long endurance and a heavy weapon load; an extension to the Specification, issued in 1949, was to build a third aircraft with three crew. As with all Royal Navy aircraft, there was also the requirement that it should occupy the minimum of hangar floor space, fit beneath the overhead beams in the hangar of an aircraft carrier, fit on to the lifts to take it up to the flight deck and then be capable of being catapulted from the ship (a capability that was becoming more necessary as aircraft became heavier). A further Admiralty requirement was a move away from aviation gasoline (AVGAS), a highly volatile fuel which could sink a ship if a spillage ignited (as occurred on board HMS *Dasher* in the Clyde during World War II). Therefore, the specification called for a gas turbine-driven engine burning aviation kerosene (AVCAT or AVTUR) or even diesel fuel. The specified option was the Armstrong Siddeley Double Mamba turboprop engine, comprising two identical side-by-side engines driving through a combined gearbox to the co-axial, contra-rotating propellers—a further advantage of which was to imbue the aircraft with the capability to cruise with one engine shut down and hence to improve its endurance greatly without much affecting the cruising speed.

There were two main contenders for the requirement, and contracts were issued to Fairey and to Blackburn each to build, in competition, two aircraft to be powered by the Double Mamba. The Fairey proposal, 'Q design', was for a two-seater aircraft with a monocoque aluminium-clad, deep fuselage, mid-fuselage-mounted mainplanes and a conventional tailplane at the base of the fin. The main wing flaps were of the Fairey-Youngman (modified Fowler) type, mounted on the inner and mid-wing section. The tricycle undercarriage with twin nose wheels allowed the aircraft to sit with the fuselage level on the ground (as opposed to at an angle for a tail wheel type). The two propellers were driven by the Double Mamba engines, the exhausts of which emerged above and behind the mainplane trailing

COURTESY PHILIP JARRETT

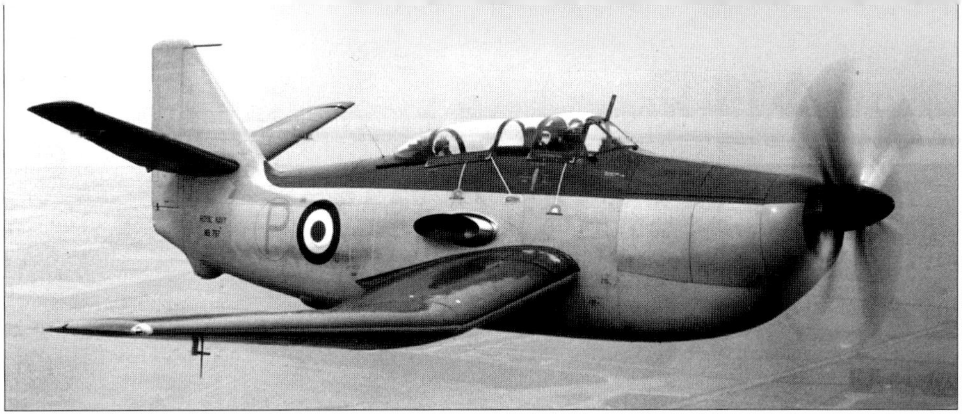

COURTESY BRIAN LOWE

COURTESY BRIAN LOWE

Right, upper: As well as the Gannet, OR.220 brought forth an imaginative design from Blackburn—the YB.1. Also powered by a Double Mamba, the aircraft apparently failed to live up to the promise of the Fairey design and was not proceeded with.
Right, lower: The Short S.B.6 Seamew, with a crew of two and a fixed undercarriage, was another contender for the A/S rôle but, although the aircraft entered production, the project was cancelled in 1957.
Below: The prototype Fairey Gannet, VR546.

edge. This won the competition and was then called the Gannet.

The other main contender, the Blackburn aircraft, was known as the YB.1. This flew, but came second in the initial assessments and so was not continued. A possible but unsuccessful anti-submarine contender—although not to the same specification—was the Short Seamew, a single-engined aircraft with a crew of two. Like a 'mini-Gannet' in some ways, it featured a mid-fin tailplane and a radome below the pilot's cockpit; the observer was accommodated over the main spar of the mainplanes. Interestingly, it was powered by a single Armstrong Siddeley Mamba engine, the double version of which would power the Gannets. The Seamew arrived in 1953 and carried out some deck trials with 700 Squadron but proved so limited when compared with the Gannet that, although twenty examples were manufactured, they were scrapped without entering front-line service.

DEVELOPMENT AND PRODUCTION

Commander Simon Askins

FAIREY Aviation produced one or two 'pre-prototypes' of their proposed new anti-submarine aircraft. These included a radically modified Firefly with a much larger engine driving contra-rotating propellers, and a variant of the short-lived Spearfish aircraft built at the end of World War II. The original engine powering the pre-prototype was a Fairey concept, designated P.24 Prince, an 'H'-configured, petrol-driven piston engine with two banks of twelve vertically opposed cylinders—a large and heavy powerplant that did not deliver the required performance. The advent of the turboprop engine was a welcome development, and the Armstrong Siddeley Double Mamba offered more power, lighter weight, higher endurance and better reliability.

The first Gannet prototype, serial number VR546, was first flown on 19 September 1949 by chief test pilot Gordon Slade from the airfield at RAF Aldermaston. Superficially, it resembled the later production Gannet but it had only two cockpits. Once it had been shown as meeting the requirement, there followed months of initial evaluation and development, delayed by a heavy landing, nose-wheel collapse and considerable damage. Early test flying, and indeed the development flying on the true prototypes, was carried out by the Fairey company test pilots Roy Moxham, Ron Gellatly (later to be the Rotodyne test pilot) and Lieutenant-Commander Peter Twiss (who went on to achieve international renown as the holder of the world air speed record in the Fairey Delta 2).

An early assessment of the Gannet's handling qualities was made in mid-1950 on a carrier deck by Peter Twiss and a small number of Royal Navy pilots. These trials, conducted on board HMS *Illustrious*,

COURTESY PHILIP JARRETT

Right: Fairey test pilot Peter Twiss prepares for a flight in the Gannet prototype. The prominent fairing extending below the cockpit sill (on both sides, and a feature of all marks of production Gannets too) was cover plating for systems wiring and ducts.
Below: Another view of VR546, parked well out of the public eye in a corner of the airfield at Aldermaston. The aircraft retains its natural metal finish and sports a rather basically shaped 'weight' in lieu of an arrester hook.

COURTESY PHILIP JARRETT

captured a 'first' for a deck landing by a turboprop aircraft (19 June 1950) and proved not only that the aircraft was a safe vehicle for this mode of operation but also that it could with confidence either be catapulted or perform free take-offs from aircraft carriers. Some handling problems were identified, particularly regarding the approach to landing, and these were exacerbated when a dummy canopy was added towards the tail to accommodate the third crew member called for by the Admiralty in a change to the specification; the new equipment envisaged, however, together with the requirement to carry

COURTESY PHILIP JARRETT

COURTESY PHILIP JARRETT

Above: Early publicity photographs of VR557, the second Gannet prototype, resplendent in its Royal Navy paint scheme. In the second image, the retractable radome is deployed and the open bomb bay doors give an indication of the generous capacity within. The starboard catapult hook can be seen just above to the hinge line of the bay door, forward.

radar and a sonobuoy receiver, did necessitate a crew of three. The extra canopy upset the airflow around the tail, especially when the aircraft was approaching the deck, as it reduced the effectiveness of the elevator and rudder. To try to overcome these difficulties, several configurations of tailplane and elevators were tried, the former even being relocated at the top of the tailfin for five flights at the end of 1951. The new shape also introduced some longitudinal and directional instability, the ultimate cure for which proved to be the introduction of 'finlets' at the mid-tailplane position. These 'fixes' appeared on all subsequent variants of the aircraft.

The early handling problems were in part also caused by the Fleet Air Arm's landing technique of

COURTESY PHILIP JARRETT

'cutting' the power on touch-down. This put the propellers into fine pitch, with a resultant loss of airflow over the tailplane and the consequent loss of authority—hence, again, the attempts at reconfiguration. The answer was to decrease, hydraulically, the incidence of the tailplane as the flaps were lowered, thus causing the nose of the aircraft to rise and giving more rearward stick movement for landing, an added benefit of which was that on overshoot, and on raising the flaps, there was no marked pitch change for the pilot to cope with on a dark and rainy night. Together with the later technique of 'flying the aircraft down to the deck' with no change in power (also used by all the jet aircraft), the modifications meant that airflow was maintained over the tail unit, restoring elevator effectiveness throughout the approach. In the event, VR546 was so dissimilar to the final design that it was never brought up to production standard and was scrapped.

Nevertheless, the second prototype aircraft, VR557, delivered in July 1950, was broadly to the design of the first. It was sent on board HMS *Theseus* to Malta, where warm-weather trials were successfully carried out at RNAS Hal Far in June 1953. Dan Carter remembers that he was on board the carrier, with 802 Squadron in Fireflies, for the trip to the Mediterranean. The Gannet was struck down into the hangar . . . and it was then discovered that it was too heavy for the lift to be able to raise it again! No

Below : WE488 was the third prototype, and the first to show three crew stations. The head-on view clearly shows the characteristic 'gull' wing of the design. Intake blanks are in place, protecting against the accidental ingestion of foreign matter.

COURTESY PHILIP JARRETT

COURTESY PHILIP JARRETT

doubt the hitch was overcome by de-fuelling the aircraft and trying again. VR557 spent a good deal of its time at A&AEE Boscombe Down as the Ministry evaluated the Gannet against the specification. Correcting various defects, including a fire in the engine bay, and visits to the Armstrong Siddeley engine factory near Bristol all took time.

A third prototype, WE488, ordered in July 1949 and delivered May 1951, was used for fitting mock-ups for the several rear cockpit designs as the Gannet was reconfigured into a three-station aircraft. The radar was a development of the ASH type (AN/APS-4) mounted in a radome which could be lowered and raised—otherwise it would hit the ground or deck during landing (as happened with XA418 of 824 Squadron in May 1957). The operator, to be located in the rear cockpit, was positioned, unusually, in a rearward-facing seat. VR557 suffered a nose wheel collapse and terminal damage after only two years' service.

Above: XJ440, the prototype Gannet Mk 3, a completely reconfigured airframe to cater for the airborne early warning rôle. This view clearly shows not only the massive radome beneath the forward fuselage but also the relocated exhaust outlets tucked beneath the wing roots. The A/S versions of the Gannet served for some five years but the AEW variant was in the front line for nearly twenty. The career of its APS-20 radar was even more impressive: this piece of kit had already taken to the air in Skyraiders, and after the Gannets were withdrawn it was installed in RAF Shackletons.
Right: WE488's third crew station was luxuriously glazed compared with the arrangement that would be adopted in production aircraft. In this photograph the mock-up radome can also clearly be seen—and the reason it had to be made retractable can be appreciated!

COURTESY PHILIP JARRETT

COURTESY GEOFF WAKEHAM

Above: VR546, the first prototype, ended its days in an undignified state, having been written off during barrier trials at RAE Bedford.
Opposite: A number of surplus Gannets were transferred to the School of Aircraft Handling at RNAS Culdrose, frequently utilising the static 'flight-deck' marked out at the Station. Here handlers—who proudly refer to themselves by the sobriquet 'chock-heads'—practised the skills and dexterity that were so vital to the safety of the actual flight-deck routine.

Once production was under way, there followed a short break in development until the final 'real' variant of the Gannet—the airborne early warning (AEW) version, designated Mk 3—was ready to be ordered in prototype form. The Fleet Air Arm had been using the Douglas Skyraider in this rôle for some years from 1953 with 849 Squadron in four flights, one for each fleet carrier. The radar in use for that aircraft was earmarked for the Gannet, but its weight, at nearly a ton, led to the realisation that the basic Gannet airframe would not accommodate it. Thus a new airframe had to be designed, albeit to much the same specification in terms of configuration, speed and endurance. The first prototype Mk 3, XJ440, was ordered in December 1954 and the first production batch of 31 aircraft in February 1956. The first flight, in XJ440, was carried out by test pilot Peter Twiss on 20 August 1958. The prototype was merely an aerodynamic test platform, and a flying test-bed for the Double Mamba 102. Unfortunately, the aircraft was lost on an engine development flight at Bristol Siddeley later that year, but deliveries of production aircraft began a few months later, in December 1958.

On completion of the Gannet's initial acceptance trials, the first production order was signed on 31 January 1951 for 100 A.S. Mk 1s for 'priority build'—to meet the emerging Soviet submarine threat. The first production aircraft, WN339, was completed in June 1953, subsequent machines arriving at the rate of one a month until early 1954, when output doubled. This delivery rate meant that Fairey could not produce all the aircraft at one plant, and some Gannets were therefore built at Hayes and others at Stockport. The Hayes Gannets were test-flown from the grass airfield at White Waltham near Maidenhead and those assembled at Stockport from Ringway Airport, Manchester.

The first two aircraft had to go to A&AEE Boscombe Down for evaluation and the CA Release to authorise military flying. This was combined with visits to RAE Bedford for ground catapult trials and arrested landings, plus visits to ships for deck trials. As was usual with a new aircraft type, A&AEE retained two airframes for many years to evaluate modifications and changes as they were cleared by the manufacturer. In the case of the Gannet, these aircraft never went into squadron service.

The facilities at RAE Bedford (at Thurleigh airfield) were unique in Britain. They included a replica of a carrier's catapult built on a steel frame about six feet above ground level, with a long ramp up to it and facing down one of the runways. Provided the wind was from approximately ahead, any naval aircraft could be catapulted, either to test new aircraft or to familiarise new pilots to the feel of the experience. And an experience it was! To achieve a flying speed of over 80 knots in a 100-foot run required considerable force, and one was really pressed into the seat-back during a launch. Should flying speed not be achieved, the aircraft would slowly sink the six feet down to the runway, from where, with full power still applied, it usually managed to get airborne.

The catapult at Bedford may have been less powerful than those on the carriers, as shown when an aircraft of 703X Flight was flown off HMS *Albion* by the unit's Senior Pilot, Lieutenant-Commander (now Admiral) Desmond Cassidi. The Gannet experienced a starboard engine failure as it was launched along the catapult, the cause of the problem later being diagnosed as fuel starvation, the fuel in the long pipe-run having been delayed by the inertia force. The cure for this was to introduce small, air-charged recuperators into the fuel pipes to ensure positive pressure throughout the launch sequence. On this occasion, the observer, a civilian from Boscombe Down, was lost. The fault had not been apparent on the Bedford catapult.

Also fitted at Bedford was an arrester wire system, again similar to those on board the carriers (and now replicated, in the form of SPRAG or PUAG systems, at many military air bases to allow arrested landings on runways). This had been set up to determine that a new aircraft could withstand the deceleration of such a landing, that the hook would not break or pull out of the airframe, and that there were no unexpected effects within the cockpit (for example, that the pilot suffered no injury and that levers and switches were stable under inertia). One aircraft, WN343, was allocated for these trials and never reached a squadron. The trials also included testing the extremes of 'off-centre' engagement acceptable for a landing. Weapons carriage was also evaluated, to cater for an aircraft returning to the ship with unexpended ordnance (everything should remain secured to the airframe and not detach and slide off the flight deck!), while the nylon barrier erected there tested airframes for both 'normal' and off-centre barrier entry and assessed any resulting damage.

In addition to the aircraft test programmes and pilot training, officers and ratings of the deck crews were trained at Bedford on procedures for catapult launches and arrested landings, and for barrier engagements. This training, combined with that offered by the School of Aircraft Handling at RNAS Culdrose, ensured that the naval aircraft handlers

COURTESY GEOFF WAKEHAM

VIA AUTHOR

were all competent in an environment where passing orders verbally was almost impossible (and hence had to be achieved by means of hand signals)

With the development of the basic airframe assessed, the Gannet was given a 'release' to allow it to enter squadron service, operate from aircraft carriers and ashore, and deliver its various weapons. In the meantime, however, because the aircraft's gestation was proving so protracted, the Admiralty decided to purchase a batch of 100 Avengers (with the petrol-fuelled Wright Cyclone

Above: XG884, a Gannet T.5, and XL472, an A.E.W.3, of 849 HQ Flight photographed over Milford Haven in the late 1960s.
Below: XA510, a T. Mk 2 trainer seen prior to its delivery to 737 Squadron. The Gannet trainers differed from the Mk 1s essentially in having their radar equipment deleted and the observer's cockpit re-fitted for dual control, facilitating which was the instructor's external periscope clearly visible here.

R.2600 engine) as an interim measure, although the Grumman aircraft did not satisfy the full requirement. These were delivered to Glasgow from the United States in early 1953 by HMS *Perseus*, were then sent on to RNAS Abbotsinch for the installation of basic British radios and then transferred to Scottish Aviation at Prestwick for conversion to A.S.4 or A.S.5 standard. This included the fitting of the ASV Mk 19 radar and an ECM fit. The aircraft did not reach squadrons until the end of 1953. At least the Avenger was a proven aircraft type, and needed no great testing for carrier clearance. The Gannet was just starting to be delivered at this time, but it would take a further year for it to be brought to a standard suitable for squadron service.

The Royal Navy now had to set up an initial receipt facility to accept all the new production aircraft on to Admiralty charge. The air station selected was RNAS Anthorn in Cumberland, known to the Navy as HMS *Hornbill*. Here each of the new Gannets was checked by a Royal Navy pilot and received modifications (including the installation of operational equipment but also 'fixes' prepared by the manufacturer to deal with problems that had arisen). From here they were allocated to squadrons and delivered by ferry crews—frequently pilots working for contractors such as Shorts. On occasion, when production was ahead of requirements, aircraft were flown up to RNAS Abbotsinch (HMS *Sanderling*) and the Holding Unit there.

Following on from the initial batch of 100 A.S.1s, the Ministry ordered 71 more aircraft in May 1952. Thereafter, the aircraft were produced in a series of developments. First came the T.1 trainer (a modified A.S.1 airframe), powered by the Double Mamba 100 which produced 2,950ehp. As the A.S.1 had proved to be somewhat underpowered, a more potent engine was developed, the Double Mamba 101, of 3,035ehp, and this was introduced for the A.S.4 variant (of which 45 were ordered), which was otherwise very similar in terms of size, performance and equipment to the A.S.1. The next development was an improved T.1 trainer designated the T.2 (but still with the 100-series engine), which in turn was

COURTESY PHILIP JARRETT

FAIREY GANNET PRODUCTION

Mark	No. built	Serial nos.	Remarks
A.S. Mk 1	172	WN, XA	All new-build
T. Mk 1	5	XA	Converted from A.S.1
T. Mk 2	36	WN, XA, XG	Converted from A.S.1
A.S. Mk 4	90	XA, XG	Mostly new-build
A.E.W. Mk 3	44	XL, XP, XR	All new-build
C.O.D. Mk 4	6	XA, one XG	Converted from A.S.4
T. Mk 5	25	XG	Eight from T.2, remainder new-build
E.C.M. Mk 6	10	XA, XG	Converted from A.S.1 and 4

Below: T. 5 XG883 on a test flight, finished in the standard training scheme of the 1950s—overall 'aluminium' with wide yellow wing and fuselage bands.
Right XA459 was built as an A.S.4 and served as such for a few years before being converted to E.C.M 6 standard in 1960. It was flown by 831 Squadron (in whose markings it is seen here) in this guise for a number of years.

superseded by the better-equipped T.5 with the uprated 101 engine. The next higher-powered variant of the Double Mamba, the 102, was already being developed by 1954 as it was known that the AEW Gannet variant would be heavier. A trial engine was fitted to A.S.1 WN345, and the 102 was to become the standard engine for the delayed Gannet A.E.W. Mk 3.

The Royal Navy had always been aware of the potential of electronic warfare in either an active mode (jamming and confusing enemy radar and radio signals) or passive mode (eavesdropping on the transmissions of others in order to analyse the power and content of messages and signals, and the direction of the transmitter). Although the existing Gannets had some capability in this field, a dedicated ECM variant was clearly required. Some A.S.1s were partially fitted, and by 1959 a batch of A.S.4s had been fully converted to the specification, resulting in the E.C.M. Mk 6.

In 1955 Fairey had both production lines running. There was no particular split in production, with A.S.1s and A.S.4s coming off both lines at the same time, while the final batch of thirteen RN T.2s was ordered at the same time as the first batch of nine T.5s. These were all built at Hayes, and flown from White Waltham. Interestingly, the A.S.1s and 4s had a relatively short service life, partly because they were overtaken by the technology offered in helicopters for anti-submarine detection and prosecution and partly because the Navy was contracting during the 1960s and 1970s and there were fewer carriers from which to operate fixed-wing aircraft. The helicopters took up less space, although they could never offer the endurance of the Gannet. Thus many of the early A.S.1 and 4 airframes were only flying for some five or six years, and fatigue was never a problem. This compares with the projected airframe life of about 30 years expected from aircraft in the early twenty-first century.

As with any aircraft, there were casualties arising from accidents or lesser incidents. Initially, any aircraft requiring major repair would go back to the manufacturer. Nevertheless, the Navy would expect to do all manner of repairs almost as soon as aircraft reached the first squadrons, and so it set up a repair facility at RNAS Donibristle (HMS *Merlin*) in Fifeshire. Designated an RN Aircraft Repair Yard (RNAY), this required that the establishment have to hand all necessary tooling, support stands, aircraft drawings and, eventually, repair jigs. It could also fit any equipment which was unavailable 'at build', such as the autopilot. Conveniently, there was an RN propeller repair shop nearby in Dundee. With the run down in the anti-submarine versions of the

D. HUDSON, COURTESY RICHARD L. WARD

Gannet, and of the Fleet Air Arm generally in the late 1950s, the repair yard at Donibristle was no longer required, and it closed in 1959.

The total number of Gannets built for all customers was 346. Various problems with the engine, together with other, unexplained occurrences, accounted for some 50–60 being written off in crashes. Some of the aircraft involved in these incidents, although repairable, were not worked on because of the excess numbers on the inventory. Of the A.E.W. Mk 3s, 22 out of the 44 built were lost to accidents or misfortune.

Not all the aircraft were 'new build': as shown in the accompanying table, many of the trainers were converted from new or re-worked A.S.1s and 4s, while the CODs and ECMs were all conversions. In addition, export orders were met by Fairey partly from new-build airframes and partly through buying back RN aircraft with low hours and reconditioning them. There was actually a surplus of RN aircraft as,

COURTESY PHILIP JARRETT

Remarkable and Versatile

Lieutenant-Commander Peter Wilkins

The Gannet A.E.W.3 was a remarkable and versatile machine. With three good men on board it was possible to achieve results that were out of all proportion to the limitations imposed by the comparatively elderly design of both the aircraft and its radar: by the time it came into service, the speed of the likely low-level threat was a challenge to the abilities and ingenuity of the AEW observers, to put it mildly.

I think the most difficult detection task I faced was during NATO exercises in the North Sea involving simulated attacks on the Netherlands by F-104s, which had a tiny radar profile when seen from ahead. We only really saw them at any distance when they altered course, and then they tended to disappear again!

Having said that, pick-up ranges of 70 to 80 miles or more could be achieved in good conditions if you got the height right, as temperature layers in the atmosphere could mask even the strongest contacts. In hot weather, even at night, a temperature inversion could complicate your best efforts. The other interesting challenge was the sea state: in rough surface conditions the sea returns on the radar extended significantly out towards the optimum detection range, limiting what could be done in the way of intercepting the targets.

Nevertheless, we usually managed very well. The trick, of course, was to see as a discrete radar return what to the uninitiated was simply another area of background noise, and to be able to track and successfully intercept it. This reminds me that my last 849 Squadron appointment was as CO of 'B' Flight in *Hermes*, in 1967–68, and that the same ship, modified for V/STOL operations, was in later years part of the Falklands Task Force, when there was no AEW cover at all. That helicopter-borne AEW rapidly developed was a credit to all concerned, but I well remember a former member of the War Cabinet saying to me, 'Ah, yes—the irreplaceable Gannet!'

Right: In terms of longevity and value for money, the APS-20 radar must surely be one of the most cost-effective systems ever to be taken into service by Great Britain's armed forces. The characteristic 'inverted mushroom' first appeared on RN Skyraiders before being transplanted to Gannets, and after 1978 it eked out its days slung beneath a handful of ancient RAF Shackletons. It was only with the introduction of the AEW Sea King helicopter fleet that this World War II-vintage search system was finally abandoned.

in mid-programme, the RNVR's 1840 and 1842 Squadrons were disbanded. All the RNVR units flying Fireflies had been scheduled to receive Gannet A.S. Mk 4s as replacements, but only the Channel Air Division actually took them on charge.

In later years, when the A.S.4s had been superseded by helicopters for anti-submarine work, half a dozen of them were converted to carrier onboard delivery (COD) aircraft, with the radar removed from the rear cockpit together with its displays etc. They were used as transports for VIP visits to carriers, or sometimes to fly operational staff to carriers for briefings. Using the aircraft's big (and now vacant) bomb bay, mail and stores could readily be accommodated too. Each of the aircraft carriers had one on board as part of the Gannet Flight, or, if unavailable, they carried an A.S.1 or 4 without modification. The COD aircraft were usually painted a uniform dark blue all over.

By the mid-1960s, and with its cancellation of CVA-01, the Navy's new fleet carrier, the Government of the day had signed the death warrant of fixed-wing shipboard aviation in the Royal Navy—or so it seemed—and the ECM task would henceforth have to be carried out by land-based aircraft. Thus 831 Squadron with their ECM Sea Venoms and Gannets moved to RAF Watton to work alongside their RAF counterparts, who were flying Canberras. Eventually the Gannets were phased out and the Navy crews were transferred to fly the Canberra in a combined RN/RAF unit, No 360 Squadron. In a final twist, in early 1966 some of the E.C.M.6s were converted back to A.S.4 standard to be used for pilot training with 849 Squadron.

The final variant of the Gannet was the airborne early warning version, the A.E.W. Mk 3, which, as explained earlier, had been numbered in the sequence in which it was expected to be produced. However, because of modifications to the radar and radome, a bigger and heavier airframe had been necessitated. With a higher all-up weight (by some 5,000 pounds), the undercarriage had to be more robust and have a longer oleo stroke—hence different wing cut-outs and undercarriage doors. The fuselage was about a foot longer than that of the A/S version—which made the fin and tailplane more effective with the longer fulcrum to the centre of lift. The tailfin was also bigger and taller than previously, to improve the aircraft's yawing stability. The deck hook was strengthened. In fact, in the event, such was the level of redesign that the Mks 3 and 4 had as little as five per cent commonality in terms of airframe components. The whole structure of the Mk 3 was different—mostly heavier and bigger—although the altered

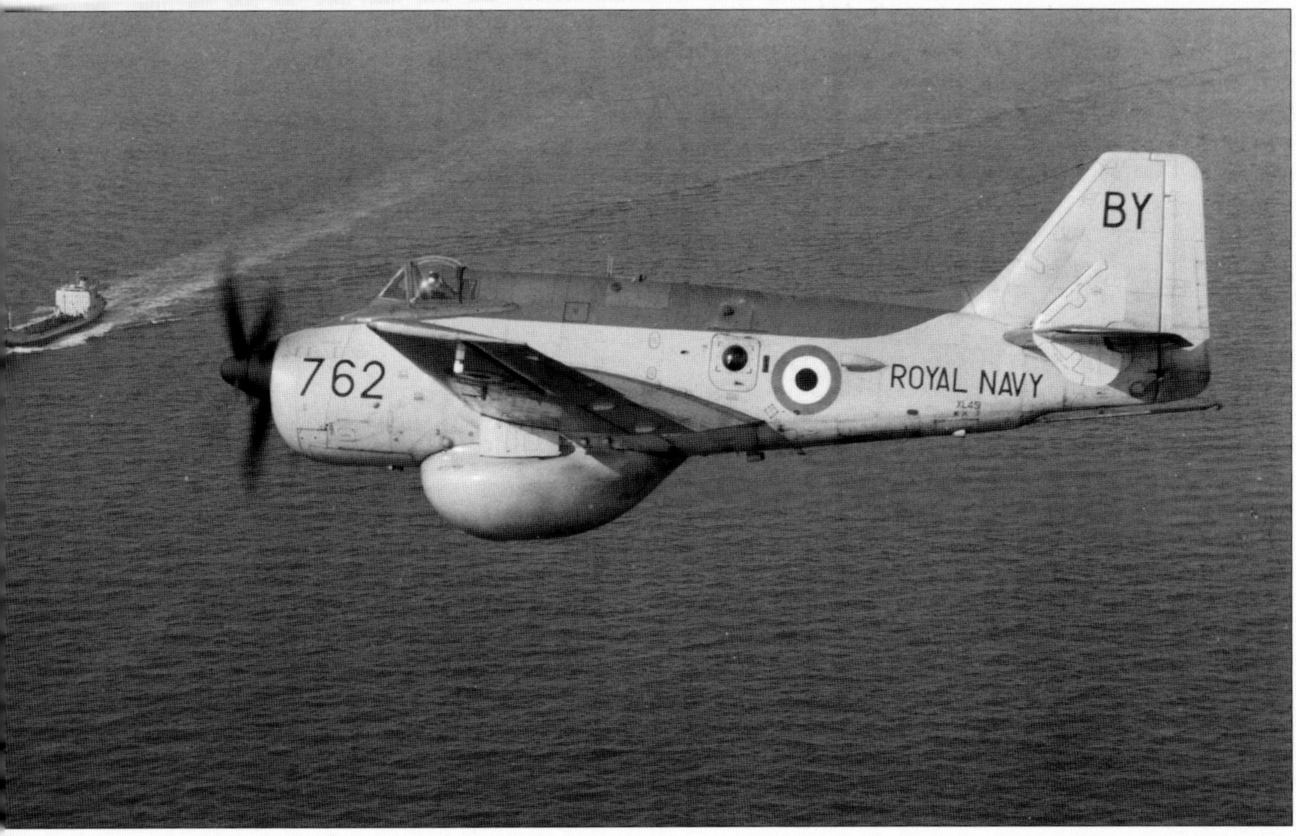

COURTESY BRIAN LOWE

aerodynamics did have the advantage that the variable-incidence tailplane was not needed and the design reverted to a fixed unit.

A more powerful, 3,875ehp Double Mamba 102 with an extra 800ehp had been flight-tested in an A.S.1 airframe (WN345) as far back as 1956. One major difference in the engine installation in the Mk 3 was that the exhaust-gas ducting, which in the Mks 1 and 4 had been taken through the fuselage and exited over the top of, and to the rear of, the wing trailing edge, was now led directly from the rear of the engines to exit below the wings, just abaft the *leading* edge. The exhaust gas—which gave a small measure of residual thrust—also now blew through the slotted flaps on the mainplane trailing edge, offering the pilot a little more control at approach speeds.

These aircraft were only to complete a twenty-year operational life because of the demise of the big aircraft carriers; they would otherwise probably have flown for at least another twenty, assuming that attrition did not overtake them. As the Gannet fleet was run down, the APS-20 radars carried in the aircraft were transplanted into RAF Shackletons, and No 8 Squadron RAF was formed to operate them. A few Royal Navy observer officers were 'loaned' to the RAF to train the necessary personnel. The Shackleton fit had a third radar screen and a third operator—but then the aircraft were expected to carry out patrols of up to twelve hours' duration. After 1978, when HMS *Ark Royal* paid off, the final APS-20F assemblies, plus the radar aerials, were handed over to the RAF to continue providing AEW information for combined operations for a further ten years—although they could not get as far as the Falklands Isles to cover the 1982 conflict!

The Falklands War proved that it was essential for the Royal Navy to have indigenous AEW in order to safeguard its ships; the only other option was to place frigates or destroyers about fifty miles away from the fleet to provide the radar cover. In the event this was soon realised by the enemy, and led to the loss of *Coventry* and *Sheffield* to missile attack. There was a concerted effort to resurrect the three most suitable Gannets from museums and elsewhere and take them to the South Atlantic, but the work required was quickly deemed too time-consuming. A rushed conversion of an ASW Sea King to carry Searchwater radar (ironically borrowed from the RAF Nimrods) proved to be a suitable successor to the venerable Gannet, although it also was too late for the combat phase of the war. This programme, however, led to the re-emergence of 849 Naval Air Squadron as the AEW centre for the Royal Navy.

Of the total number of Gannets built, over 70 were for export. Australia ordered 36, West Germany (before reunification) bought 16 and Indonesia bought 22. The Australians accepted the first version of the aircraft, the A.S.1, but Germany waited for the soon-to-be-developed, higher-powered A.S. Mk 4.

The RAN ordered 33 A.S.1s and three T. Mk 2 trainers. These were delivered in 1955 and retired in 1967. They retained their Royal Navy XA and XG serial numbers except for XD898, which was a late order. The aircraft did not pass through the Royal Navy acceptance procedure. One T.2, XG888, was repurchased by the RN in 1970 and brought back from Australia on board HMS *Victorious* for use by 849 Squadron until training finally ceased in 1978. It was sent back again in 1995 for the Nowra Naval Aviation Museum. The crews of 816 and 817 Squadrons trained with the Royal Navy at RNAS Culdrose, initially on RN aircraft but on their own Gannets once these had been delivered. They then moved to RNAS Eglinton for operational training. Half of the Australian aircraft were shipped out on HMAS *Melbourne* and the remainder were sent direct from Fairey UK to Fairey (Bankstown) by freighter.

West Germany, a member of NATO, had formed a naval air arm, the *Bundesmarine*, and to equip it ordered fifteen Gannet A.S. Mk 4s and a single T.5, having purchased also the Armstrong Whitworth Sea Hawk fighter. The Gannets came from a cancelled RN order, and while awaiting their own aircraft the Germans were loaned some of the Royal Navy A.S.4s so that training could get under way. The pilots were taught by Fairey at White Waltham airfield in 1956 and then spent time at RNAS Eglinton to work up.

COURTESY BILL HARRISON

COURTESY PHILIP JARRETT

Above: The single Gannet trainer supplied to the *Bundesmarine*, with bomb bay doors open and one propeller feathered. During training at Eglinton, one of the German pilots was able to 'celebrate' the dropping of a 1,000-pound bomb on 'British' soil!
Left: XA331, a Gannet A. S. Mk 1 for the Royal Australian Navy. The aircraft is assigned to 816 Squadron and the identifying tail letter denotes HMAS *Melbourne*, the receving carrier.
Right, upper: A West German Gannet on display at the 1958 Farnborough Air Show. One imagines that the presentation would be rather more elaborate nowadays!
Right, lower: The RAN's XA332 lands on board HMAS *Melbourne*. The short-lived tail code 'Y' can just be seen; this was changed to 'M' in 1956—from about which time also the red centres of the British Type 'D' roundels began to be replaced with the characterstic 'bounding kangaroo' emblem.

RICHARD L. WARD

COURTESY BILL HARRISON

COURTESY KEITH CHADBOURN

The aircraft were retired in 1967. Indonesia had also formed a naval air arm—the *Angkatan Laut Republik Indonesia*—following the country's independence in the early 1950s. It purchased twenty A.S.4s and two T.5s. To meet the Indonesian order, Fairey bought back from the Ministry of Supply a number of low-life Royal Navy A.S.1 airframes, refurbished them to A.S.4 standard and then trained the aircrew on two T.5s at White Waltham. Fairey also sent engineering and flying instruction support teams, led by ex-RN pilot Keith Chadbourn, to Indonesia to assist with the aircraft's introduction to squadron service there from early 1960.

One Gannet, WN365, the T.2 prototype, was brought up to T.5 standard, was used by Fairey for the training and was eventually repurchased by the RN with the new serial number XT572. It flew with 849 Squadron until 1978 and was eventually sold, still in flying condition, to an American preservation group.

SPECIFICATIONS

FAIREY GANNET Mks 1–6

Manufacturer:	The Fairey Aviation Company Ltd, Hayes, Middlesex. Production/conversion work at Hayes and at Heaton Chapel (Cheshire).
Chief Designer:	H. E. Chaplin.
Powerplant:	One Armstrong Siddeley Double Mamba 100 of 2,950ehp or (Mk 4) 101 of 3,035ehp or (Mk 3) 102 of 3,875ehp.
Dimensions:	Length overall 43ft (13.11m) or (Mk 3) 44ft (13.41m); wing span 54ft 4in (16.56m) spread, 19ft 11in (5.82m) folded; height 13ft 9in (4.19m) wings spread or folded; wing area 483.0 sq ft (44.87m^2).
Weights:	14,070lb (6,360kg) empty; 21,600lb (9,800kg) or (Mk 3) 25,000lb (11,350kg) max. loaded.
Armament:	Up to 2,500lb (1,135kg) of stores and/or ordnance in bomb bay; max. external load 1,000lb (450kg). Mk 3 unarmed.
Performance:	Max. speed 360kts (415mph, 666kph) or (Mk 3) 280kts (320mph, 520kph); service ceiling 25,000ft (7,600m); max. range (standard fuel, cruise) 520nm (600 miles, 970km), or (Mk 3) 600nm (700 miles, 1,120km); typical endurance 4.5hrs or (Mk 3) 5.5hrs.

Left; Personnel from the Indonesian Navy pose for the camera during their conversion course at White Waltham in 1959. Right, upper: XA327, an A.S.1 issued to 724 Squadron RAN for training after brief service in the front line. 'NW' denotes NAS Nowra, the Australian Navy's principal air training establishment. Right; lower: 'UA+106', an A.S.4 purchased by the West German Navy and now preserved at the German Air Force Museum at Berlin-Gatow. This aircraft is believed originally to have borne the code 'UA+110'.
Below: Past and present: A Sea King A. E. W. Mk 2A hovers over Gannet Mk 3 XL500 during the latter's post-retirement sojourn at RNAS Culdrose in the 1990s.

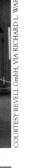

BILL HARRISON

COURTESY REVELL GmbH, VIA RICHARD L. WARD

COURTESY GEOFF WAKEHAM

Skwaduraks Seratus . . . *Keith Chadbourn*

The first Indonesian Gannet student flew in July 1959 at White Waltham and the training continued until mid-1960. There was only one mishap: Sub-Lieutenant Budiharto in A.S.1 AS16 performed a wheels-up landing on the airfield at night and the aircraft was written off. Normally the Gannet could stand such a landing and be rebuilt, since airframe damage was usually confined to nosewheel doors, bomb bay doors and radome, but in this case it was a grass airfield in autumn and the build-up of soft earth and turf as the aircraft slid a long caused some of the frames to buckle. In any case it was good business, because the Indonesians bought another one!

I left for Sourabaya in January 1960 to start setting up the Indonesian base and the training programmes preparatory to the arrival of the first two aircraft. The Indonesian Navy had no air arm at that time and they bought all their equipment through Fairey Aviation—runway caravans, sweepers, Queen Marys, the lot. Quite why a comparatively poorly equipped country like Indonesia should decide to start a Fleet Air Arm with such a complex aircraft as the Gannet, and pay fairly heavily for it when other nations were offering aircraft for free, I shall never know, but I am sure the company was grateful.

A Headquarters Flight was set up as an administrative base until sufficient pilots and observers had been trained and until there were enough aircraft. The first two aircraft, A.S.4 AS01 and T.5 LA01, arrived in February 1960; AS02, the second Mk 4, and LA17, the second T.5, arrived in early April. At about this time LA01 was re-serialled LA18. The Indonesians were very fond of changing the numbers of their aircraft: whether this was to confuse the enemy I know not, but it certainly confused me. The numbers changed again in September when the 'AS' and 'LA' prefixes were dropped and AS01 became 101 and so on, LA17 and 18 becoming 117 and 112, respectively.

The mission was a great success, with the exception of the loss of one aircraft, 103, and its pilot in July 1960, when it crashed following a unsuccessful single-engine overshoot. The ALRI's first squadron, No 601, was formed from the old Headquarters Flight on 1 December 1960 with one T.5 (118) and five A.S.4s (101, 102, 104, 105 and 106). Nos 107 and 100 had arrived on 30 November and were undergoing checks before acceptance test-flights.

In true Indonesian fashion, the number 601 did not survive for long and the Squadron was re-formed in July 1961 as *Skwaduraks Seratus* (Skwad = 'Squadron', Ur = Udars or 'Air', AKS = Anti Kepal Selam or 'Anti-Submarine', Seratus = 'One Hundred'). It had all the available aircraft, 101–110 excluding 103, and 117 and 118, the two trainers. Aircraft 111, 112, 113 and 114 were added as they arrived in November and December, and the Squadron was still going strong when I left Indonesia in January 1962. Gannets 115 and 116, the last two A.S.4s, had not then arrived, and in view of the increasing tension between Great Britain and Indonesia (and also between the Netherlands and Indonesia) it is perhaps surprising that they were allowed to be exported.

The ensuing Confrontation was the source of some amazement to us, for although the Indonesians were wont to adopt a belligerent attitude for foreign consumption, although the cinemas were for ever showing films of the Indonesian armed forces training (and, of course, winning), and although the streets of the cities were festooned with garish posters depicting brown men doing unspeakable things to white men, we found them to be a remarkably happy and peaceable people.

The Confrontation sounded the death-knell of the Gannet in that part of the world. No spares had been delivered for about a year by the time the last mission member left towards the end of 1964, and it is thought that the aircraft stopped flying some time late the following year.

Below: XL450 was the very last Gannet to be reconditioned for service in the Fleet Air Arm. It is seen here on 16 August 1974 over the Somerset countryside on its first test flight following its upgrading, in the hands of Westland's Chief Test Pilot Keith Chadbourn.

. . . From Blackbushe to Sourabaya *Dan Carter*

I joined the Royal Navy in January 1950 as an aviation cadet on a short-service commission (eight years), and by the summer of 1957 I was serving in 700 (Trials) Squadron at Ford. I converted to the Gannet there in July, and from then until mid-December I was engaged in the aircraft's UHF radio trial, flying mostly from RAF Watton. The two aircraft used were XA412 and WN426, and about 160 hours were flown in total.

At the end of the year I left the Navy, and in February 1958 I joined Airwork as a staff pilot at St David's in Pembrokeshire, flying Sea Venoms for the Air Direction School at Kete. In January 1960 I was asked to join a Gannet ferry to Indonesia, which country had bought eighteen aircraft to equip its naval air arm. Two aircraft at a time were to be flown out, the first pair led by Squadron Leader Joe Tyzko, of Polish origin, who at the time was Chief Test Pilot at Airwork.

We collected the aircraft at White Waltham, flew to Blackbushe for customs clearance, and set off on 28 January. I had with me as crew Taff James and Lieutenant Yusuf of the Indonesian Navy, and the route flown was Blackbushe–Nice–Brindisi (night stop)–Athens–Beirut (night stop)–Baghdad–Bahrein (night stop)–Sharjah–Karachi (night stop)–Delhi (night stop; unfortunately Joe burnt out his engine on starting here, so I went on alone)–Lucknow–Calcutta (night stop)–Rangoon–Bangkok (night stop)–Butterworth–Singapore (night stop)–Djakarta–Sourabaya. The total flying time was 46 hours.

Arriving at Djakarta, we got the full treatment, greeted by a high-powered reception party—the head of the Navy, all the military attachés, newsreel cameras, the Press and pretty girls with bouquets—and this was followed by a sit-down lunch, all the while with Taff and I still in our scruffy flying overalls! Eventually we got away and flew to Sourabaya, arriving on 7 February.

The first three ferries were made with bomb-bay overload fuel tanks but from the fourth the Gannets flew without them. I flew on the fourth and subsequent ferries, made between August 1960 and January 1961, for which the crews comprised myself and Pete Aplin in one aircraft and Dave Parker and Bob Manners in the other. The route for these flights was Hurn (customs)–Dijon–Nice–Rome–Brindisi–Athens–Izmir–Nicosia–Damascus–Baghdad–Basra–Bahrain–Sharjah–Jiwani–Karachi–Jodhpur–Delhi–Lucknow–Calcutta–Akyab–Rangoon–Mergui–Butterworth–Singapore–Djakarta–Sourabaya. It was on the first of these that I handed over my aircraft in Djakarta as the

DAN CARTER

Above: Dan Carter takes a break at a stopover during one of the ferry flights to Indonesia.

Below: A manufacturer's publicity photograph showing two of the Gannet A.S.4s and (centre) a T.5 trainer supplied to Indonesia. In the event, the service careers of these aircraft were brief, the supply of spares being withheld as a result of the Confrontation of the early 1960s.

COURTESY KEITH CHADBOURN

Indonesians wanted to put it on display in the local park. Hence I found myself in the cockpit working the brakes as we were towed through the streets of the city to the park. It was quite fraught, as there was no towing arm and the Gannet was merely connected to a rope and pulled along. Especially hazardous was the railway level crossing!

It was on one of these ferries that one engine in my aircraft suffered from excessive oil consumption and could only be used for take off and climb to height, whereupon it had to be shut it down and we had to complete the flight on the one good Mamba—all the way from Rangoon to Sourabaya.

The last three ferries were flown between 10 August 1961 and 2 February 1962, with Ken Wilson and Bob Manners in one aircraft and myself and Pete Aplin in the second. The route was that taken for the second flights except that the Karachi–Calcutta leg took in Ahmedabad, Nagpur and

Above, below and opposite: Delivering the Indonesian Gannets to the customer was a triumph of planning and logistics, and, for the ferry crews, an eye-opening experience; such a venture would be inconceivable today. These four photographs wre taken at various stopovers during one of the flights and show (above) an engine start at Athens, (below) refuelling at Mergui, (opposite, top) a scene at Sharjah and (opposite, bottom) refuelling at Jiwani.

Gaya and on the eighth and ninth we flew to Ankara and from there to Diyabakir and on to Baghdad. Before we left we were told to night-stop in Ankara, and that we would be handled by Turkish Airlines. Sure enough, on landing we were met by the airline representative and taken to a hotel in town, and we requested transport the next morning at 0630. A Volkswagen bus was there at the appointed time. We were a little late, and rushed, and unfortunately Bob Manners didn't duck quite low enough, caught the top of his head on the door frame and lifted up the top of this scalp. There was blood everywhere. He was stitched up at the American Hospital, but he was unable to get his flying helmet on for several days. When we were ready once more to depart, we informed Turkish Airlines, who, taking no chances, sent a 42-seater bus to pick us up.

Generally speaking, the trips went well, and there was very little unserviceability except for minor hiccups—understandable after nearly two weeks of hard flying with little or no maintenance. However, by the time we got to Sourabaya I don't think any of the aircraft were fully serviceable.

POWERPLANT

Commander Simon Askins

THE Armstrong Siddeley Mamba engine was developed in the late 1940s without a specific aircraft to power. It was proposed as a twin powerplant for a 'new aircraft type' and by 1949 had been offered as a combined, side-by-side assembly, first as the Twin then as the Double Mamba. This was specified as the preferred engine for the two contenders for the Admiralty specification GR.17 M/45 for a new anti-submarine aircraft and was built into both the Fairey Gannet and the Blackburn YB.1 demonstrators. Armstrong Siddeley was absorbed by Bristol to become the Bristol Siddeley Engine Company, but under both names use was made of the airfield facility at Bitteswell, near Bristol.

The basic engine comprised a ten- stage, axial-flow compressor driven by a two-stage turbine unit. The annular combustion chamber had 24 burners. In the Double Mamba, the two engines drove through a common gearbox, with drives to an auxiliary gearbox which powered the ancillaries whether one or two engines were running. The power required was set by the pilot, who had one throttle per engine but no rpm lever. Speed was predetermined and reached by mid-throttle setting, and maintained automatically by the pitch control unit (PCU).

Each engine unit had its own oil supply, which was combined with that controlling the PCU. There was, however, a separate feathering pump with its own oil supply to each propeller unit, and this operated the 'feather and brake' function. The oil supply to the PCU was led through and between the shafts via annular cavities and ports, one side moving a piston to 'coarse' and the other to 'fine'. The movement of this piston was also limited by the 'pitch stops', allowing 'fully fine' for starting and ground idle, a mid-position for 'flight idle', and the fully feathered position.

The propeller blades were manufactured from forged duralumin alloy. Because of the greater all-up

COURTESY HELEN CLARKE

COURTESY REVELL GmbH, VIA RICHARD L. WARD

COURTESY REVELL GmbH, VIA RICHARD L. WARD

Opposite: Starting engines: an 847 Squadron Gannet A.S.1 with its rear propeller spinning as the starboard Mamba bursts into life. The smoke visible comes from the cartridge starter, of course, not the engine proper.
Above: A close inspection of the chin intake of an A.S.4 (left) and a view of the powerplant with the engine panels removed (right) reveal the 'Double' nature of the Mamba turboprop.
Below: A lashed-down XL497 running up its engines on board HMS *Ark Royal* during a performance check.

weight of the Gannet Mk 3 and that aircraft's higher engine power, the propeller diameter was increased from about 14 feet to about 16 feet. Propeller speed was at a ratio of 1:10 of engine speed, hence at cruise speed the engines would run at 15,000rpm and the propellers at 1,500rpm.

COURTESY PHILIP JARRETT

COURTESY PHILIP JARRETT

DOUBLE MAMBA VARIANTS

D no.	ehp	rpm	Weight (lb)
100	2,950	15,000	2,800
101	3,035	15,000	2,800
102	3,875	15,000	3,060

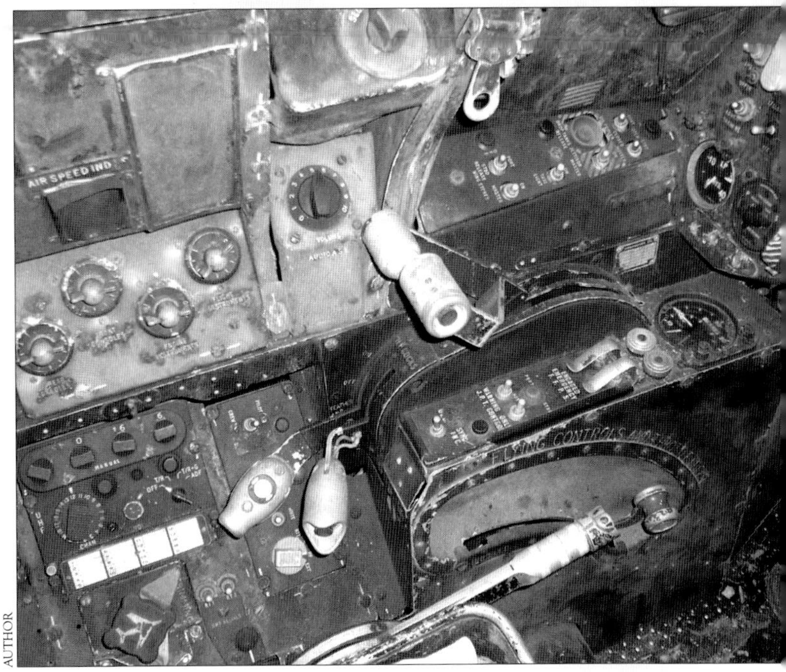

AUTHOR

Starting the Gannet A.S.1 was usually achieved by cartridge. Two were carried, and both were almost invariably needed for a start. The port engine drove the front propeller anti-clockwise, the starboard drove the rear propeller clockwise; either could be started first. The technique was to select the low-pressure (LP) fuel cock 'On', unfeather the port engine, select the high-pressure (HP) fuel cock 'On' and then to press the starter. The cartridge fired and the engine accelerated up to about 4,500rpm, light-up occurring at around 2,000rpm. If it failed to achieve self- sustaining speed, the HP cock was selected 'Off' and the engine wound down. As it reached 1,200rpm, the HP cock was moved to the 'On' position again, and the starter was pressed once again. The second cartridge fired at about 1,000rpm and the engine accelerated away to self-sustaining ground idle at 9,000rpm.

Left: A Gannet A.E.W.3 of 'B' Flight, 849 Squadron, about to touch down on *Ark Royal*.
Above right: The left side of the Gannet A.S.1's cockpit, showing the HP cocks and the power select levers.
Below: An 847 Squadron Gannet A.S.1 starts up—starboard engine first—at RAF Nicosia, late 1957.

The second engine could then be started by 'windmilling' it from the first. Having checked that the brake pressure had built up and the aircraft was secure, the running engine could be opened up to 15,000rpm and take-off power applied. To perform the start, the procedure was to move the HP cock to 'On', to release the propeller brake and then press the re-light button; the rpm built up to 9,000 as the fuel ignited. The power could then be increased to flight-idle while checks were made of all temperatures and oil pressures, after which both engines could be returned to ground idle.

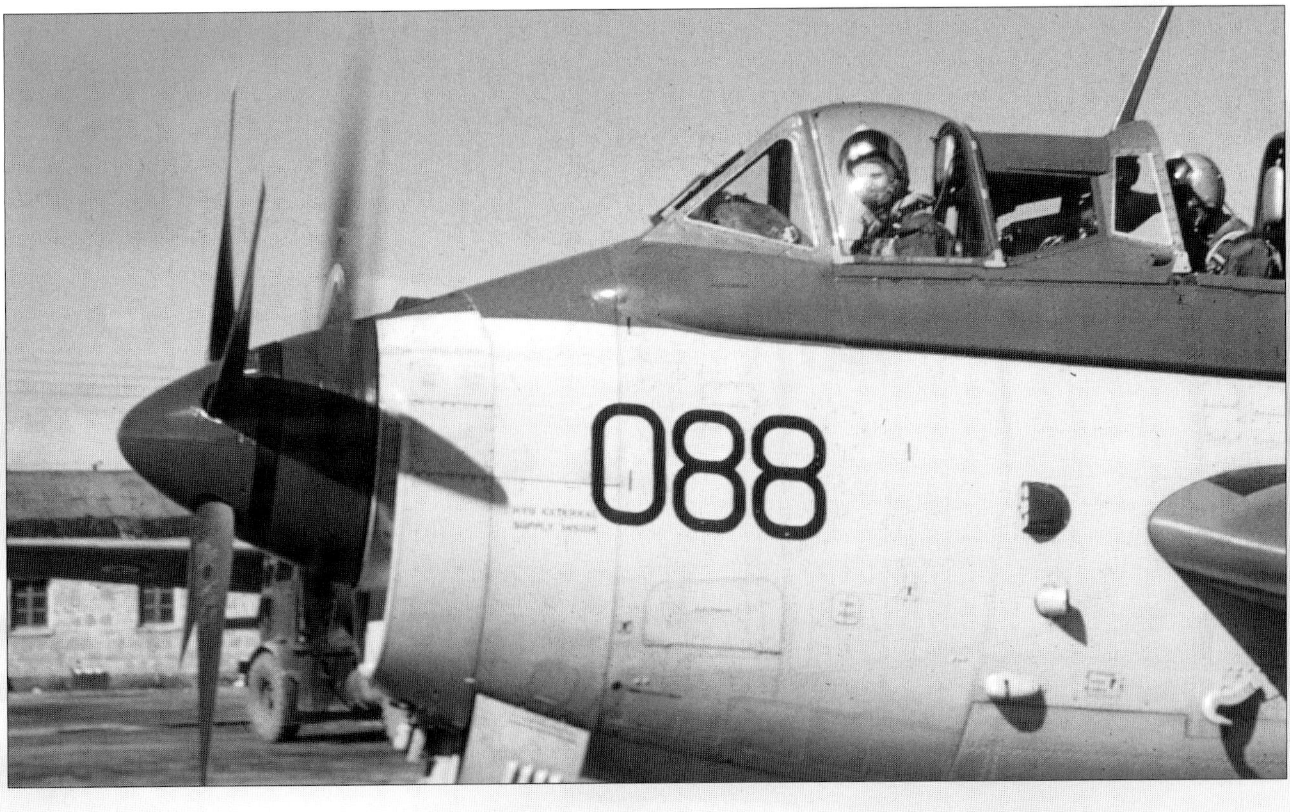

COURTESY HELEN CLARKE

An alternative method of starting–although one infrequently used—was to utilise a compressed-air supply to run the starter on the first engine. Again, it would be taken to 4,500rpm and became self-sustaining. Thereafter the procedure was as for a cartridge start.

There was a problem with the early Gannets in that in cold weather (as frequently found in Northern Ireland) the first cartridge would not have enough power to wind the engine up to self-sustaining speed and a second cartridge would then need to be fired. The enterprising Air Engineering Officer of 820 Squadron worked out that by placing the strop end of a rope around the front propeller and winding it around the boss of the propeller, and then having four strong sailors running away with the rope end at 90 degrees to the aircraft, the engine could be given an initial 1,000rpm or so before the rope end detached itself. At this point the Crew Chief gave the pilot a 'thumbs up' and the pilot fired the cartridge, whereupon the engine would start perfectly. The potential for getting this wrong was always there, and inevitably it did one day when the Chief gave the thumbs-up too early! No one was injured, but the practice was then forbidden (but remembered—just in case).

The Gannet Mk 3 was different in that it used a Palouste low-pressure air starter. This, in effect, was a small jet engine powering a compressor and was in use for a number of RN aircraft. The Palouste again enabled the engine to accelerate to the usual 4,500rpm to run itself and had the advantage that it could be carried underwing by a Gannet which could thereby start itself (or any other compatible aircraft, for that matter) when ashore. Gannet observers were qualified to start and run the Palouste in case regular ground crew were unavailable. The communications version of the Gannet, the COD, was a converted A.S.4 and thus cartridge started, so that it was unlikely to be stranded in a far-off airfield. As an emergency starting method, a running Gannet could be stationed ahead of the one to be started and its power gradually increased to allow one propeller on the second aircraft to windmill up to a speed sufficient to open the HP cock and enable the re-light button to be depressed in order to achieve a start. Mishandled, however, this could result in an overheated engine.

COURTESY BRIAN LOWE

Opposite: An 849 'A' Flight Gannet A.E.W.3 lashed down on board HMS *Centaur* in 1961. The propellers are both in the fully feathered position, although the strop to prevent them from rotating—normally fitted on parked aircraft—is not present.
Right and below: XG798 of 831 Squadron prepares for take-off. In the upper photograph, the propellers are unfeathered and facing the airstream. Below, the pilot has started up, the observer is about to clamber aboard and a line maintenance rating is about to remove the port chock. The concavity in the bomb bay doors of the anti-submarine and trainer Gannets permitted the main undercarriage to be lowered freely if for some reason these doors could not be closed (for example, in the event of a problem with the aircraft's hydraulics).

COURTESY BRIAN LOWE

COURTESY BRIAN LOWE

FROM THE COCKPIT

Commander Simon Askins

I REMEMBER walking out to a Gannet for the first time. It did look somewhat daunting, and the immediate contemplation was rather like that of climbing a block of flats: for someone more used to having his personal ladder with which to mount his jet plane, this was something else entirely. With the lowest of the push-in footholds some five feet above ground level, I thought that perhaps one was meant to spring at the side of the aircraft in 'Garfield' fashion and cling there while scrabbling for a foothold. However, my instructor, Lieutenant Hughes, then pointed out the nattily stowed footstep bar which, when lowered, gave an extra three lower steps.

The first thing any new pilot had to learn was with which foot to start the ascent towards the cockpit—left for the Mk 4 and right for the A.E.W. Mk 3. The footholds, embedded in the fuselage, were so spaced that, rather like mounting a horse, if one put the wrong foot into the stirrup one ended up facing backwards! The A.S.4 and T.5 had the let-down step with three rungs, followed by five hand/foot cut-outs in the aircraft side to give access to the front two cockpits. Once there, the pilot was about ten feet off the ground—a point to be borne in mind when approaching to land. The Mk 3 cockpit was even further away, its let-down steps being followed by seven cut-outs! Up there, the roomy cockpit awaited, with a good-sized seat. The seat held a dinghy pack and parachute, and was reasonably well padded—enough to make a four-hour flight just about bearable. The control column was conventional, comprising a floor-pivoted stick with operating buttons on it rather than a yoke where just the top moved for aileron control.

The pilot's instrument panel was again very conventional and owed little to technology as it had

RICHARD L. WARD

more or less the same instruments as did the earlier Firefly. There was a standard 'blind flying' panel in the centre with artificial horizon, turn-and-slip indicator, altimeter, airspeed indicator, compass and rate-of-climb and -descent indicator. Instrument flying practice was carried out in the T.5 trainer version of the Gannet. For this, the pilot under test or instruction would sit in the middle cockpit, which could have a black-out hood inside the canopy to put the student in the dark. This cockpit had a full set of duplicate flying and engine controls and was normally occupied by the instructor, who had a small periscope above the hood so that he could have some forward visibility.

The engine controls comprised a pair of throttles, high-pressure fuel cut-off cocks, and buttons to operate the feathering mechanism for the propellers. The engine instruments were randomly placed on the panel, although the instruments were paired for easy monitoring. The layout in the Mk 3 was somewhat improved.

All marks of the aircraft had a tricycle undercarriage which allowed the aircraft to sit with its fuselage almost horizontal, not at the sometimes steep angle associated with tail-wheel types such as the Avenger or Skyraider. It also prevented the aircraft tipping on to its propeller if it stopped abruptly. Another advantage of this layout was that it considerably improved pilot visibility when taxying as the engine was then below him.

The nosewheel assembly was of the long, spindly variety and always provided interest when it collapsed, fell off or behaved like a demented supermarket trolley wheel. It was an oleo assembly with a double wheel at the axle end and a pre-shortening mechanism, and the whole unit was free-castoring,

DAVID HOBBS

Left: The pilot's cockpit of the Gannet C.O.D. Mk 4. In the gun sight position above the panel are VHF and UHF homer dials, with TACAN and Rad Alt below. The four medium-size dials below the panel proper show engine oil temperature and pressure, and above these on the right are the rpm dials and, higher again, the twin jpt dials. The TACAN selector is immediately in front of the stick, and the stick itself has (guarded) release switches for the 'G-dropper'. Right: The front cockpit instrument panel of an A.E.W.3. The instruments of the blind flying panel—ASI, height, speed, horizon—are situated within the broad, white-painted line. To the right, the engine instruments are in pairs—from top to bottom, percentage power, oil temperature, percentage rpm, oil temperature amd oil pressure. Off to the right are the fuel contents gauge (upper) and fuel flow meter and above these are the three 'doll's-eyes' for wing fold (top), autopilot and oxygen.The dial to the left of the oil pressure gauges is the Violet Picture homer.

RICHARD L WARD

centrally biased by a cam. The Gannet lacked nosewheel steering—which did lead to some problems manœuvring on a wet deck (and even on a dry one at times). Thus, the aircraft on the ground was steered by means of differential braking on its main wheels. Taxying on grass was very difficult as the nosewheel was reluctant to turn, and the pilot would have to rely on occasional pieces of hardstanding upon which to change direction. However, there was almost no tendency for shimmy when operating from grass, although this was of little benefit to the Fleet Air Arm, who normally operated from concrete runways or steel decks.

On the flight deck, the mainwheel brakes were not sufficiently responsive for accurate taxying, so, almost invariably, a nose steering arm had to be attached. This was tended by a brave aircraft handler who was positioned about six feet in front of two high-speed propellers and then proceeded to walk backwards across what was a uneven surface. Amazingly, there is only one recorded accident of a handler being hit by a propeller—that of an A.S.4, XA413, on board *Ark Royal* in 1956.

There were obvious differences between taking off from a shore base and taking off while at sea. Taking off from an airfield posed no problems. Half flap (20 degrees) was usually employed for a lightly loaded aircraft and full flap (40 degrees) when a weapons load was carried. The aircraft was held on the brakes as the engines were run up to full power. Once rolling, the aircraft did not tend to change heading unless there were a strong crosswind, in which circumstances differential wheel braking or the application of rudder (or both) would readily keep it straight. The unstick speed was between 70 and 80 knots. Once the aircraft was airborne, the undercarriage was raised immediately—as it always was when leaving a carrier. There was a slight trim change as the flaps were raised. Take-off could on occasion be more exciting than expected, as Paul Greenwood relates on page 41.

Gannets could depart from a carrier by means of a 'free take-off' if there were enough clear deck for the run from stern to bow. This could even be undertaken with the ship at anchor, provided there was some breeze down the deck. This was useful if the main boilers of the ship happened to be shut down and there no steam was available for the catapults. The contra-rotating propellers, with the torque effect

Left: Aircrew access to the Gannet cockpits could be from either side, though on the early marks (as on this C.O.D. Mk 4) stripes helpfully drawing attention to the footholds, taking the form of a diamond, were present on the starboard side only.
Below: The Mk 3 had vertical lines to indicate destinations for the feet, together with the usual dire warnings highlighting things not to be stepped on. This is XL482, re-registered for new owners in the United States, where Hamilton Standard Propellers would employ it in a trials programme.

COURTESY GEOFF WAKEHAM

COURTESY BRIAN LOWE

from one cancelling out that from the other, made for a much easier take-off than had been the case with the Avenger or Skyraider. HMS *Ark Royal* at Malta had her Gannets, and also her AEW Skyraiders, carry out free take-offs whilst the ship was at anchor on one occasion. A slight tail wind posed torque/directional problems for the Skyraider, with its single propeller and associated problems of asymmetry as full power could not be applied until a certain ground speed was reached and the rudder

Above: Gannet A.S.1 WN353 from 700 Squadron 'C' Flight makes a free take-off from a carrier during trials in 1959.
Below: Lieutenant Vic Sirett of 812 Squadron makes the first catapult take-off from a ship in harbour by a Gannet. HMS *Eagle*, Grand Harbour, Malta, July 1956.

became fully effective–which was some way down the deck. In contrast the Gannets, with the benefit of contra-rotating propellers, had no such problems and full power could be applied once the brakes had been released. Full flap was generally used when flying off from a carrier.

Downwind Pre-Flight *Lieutenant-Commander Paul Greenwood*

I had one exciting moment—in 831 Squadron at RAF Watton. The night of 24 November 1965 I was briefed as No 2 for an hour of night flying, to include a practice diversion to a nearby RAF station but to start with a session of formation flying from a stream take-off. My observer, Lieutenant Nick Gent, and I walked out to our E.C.M.6 (XG797) and carried out our pre-flight check. It was my habit to hang my helmet on the bottom of the ladder and proceed round the aircraft in a clockwise direction; the significance of that will be explained in a moment.

We strapped in, started up, taxied out and lined up on the runway. The leader rolled, and five seconds later so did I. During the roll, I suspected that I had unconsciously applied some rudder, because as I retracted the undercarriage and turned to follow the leader, I noticed that the turn-and-slip ball was not in the centre. So I moved the rudder appropriately. There was then a big bang, and something passed over my head and hit the observer's canopy, which shattered. I called a 'Mayday' and continued in a wide circle to avoid the Type 82 radar, Married Quarters, Station HQ and the groundcrews' accommodation blocks. Fortunately, the single runway was still clear so I landed, rolled to the end, turned off and shut down.

Later investigation showed that all the cowling panels had been removed at the request of an inspection team from RNAS Yeovilton and that, when they were replaced, the fasteners between the top and bottom panels on the port side had been shut correctly but the hooks that engaged pins on the back of the intake fairing had not been fully closed. As I had walked round, in the dusk, I had approached the slightly raised panel from the 'downwind' side and as a result I had not seen it. Taking off with inadvertent skid had kept the panel tight, but when I corrected it the airflow got under the panel and tore the double panel off the aircraft along the upper 'piano hinge' and it landed in the car park of the radar installation. There were no injuries and little damage—except to the Gannet. It was all very exciting at the time, and, as they say these days, lessons were learned.

Below: Gannet E.C.M.6 XG797 under a later tenancy—that of 849 Squadron HQ Flight, at Brawdy.

RICHARD L. WARD

VIA AUTHOR

COURTESY PHILIP JARRETT

The catapult launch was another matter. The method was in principle very simple: hook a launch wire to the front of the aircraft, hold it back until you have launch pressure in the catapult, apply full power to the engines, release the holdback—and off it goes. However, the set-up with a ship's catapult did require the aircraft to be exactly centred on the track, and this was achieved by the technically simple concept of having a series of laterally driven rollers under each main wheel, the speed of rotation of each decreasing towards the centre. The other proviso for naval aircraft was that the wings had to be spread and locked! This was confirmed by 'dolls-eye' indicators in the cockpit, a visual inspection through wing cut-outs where there were indicator lights, and a visual indicator which moved flush with each wing surface when correctly spread. The system was not infallible, as was discovered in 1968 on board HMS *Hermes* off Okinawa when a Gannet Mk 3 of 'A' Flight 849 Squadron had its port mainplane fold on the catapult run, with the result that the aircraft ditched into the sea and the crew were lost. The additional tragedy there was that one of the observers had been on board XL451 two days previously when the aircraft had bolted from a night deck landing and crashed ahead of the ship, although in this instance all the crew had been saved.

The other hazard was that, should the flaps be moved while the wings were spreading, there would be terrible damage to the linkages which controlled the flaps and ailerons. There was an interlock to prevent the flaps moving with the wings folded, but no safeguards while they were in motion. Moving up the deck towards the catapult, the pilot always spread the wings and then lowered the flaps in order to check them and to set them for take-off. Hence the danger existed that he might try them too early.

The holdback had then to be attached. This was a simple device consisting of a split cylinder into which fitted a tongue with a 'T' at the end. The 'T' was gripped by cut-outs in the cylinder and held in

Left: A.E.W.3 XL471 about to launch from HMS *Eagle*, January 1972. The holdback is clearly visible.
Below: Clouds of steam engulf A.E.W.3 XP199 as it prepares to depart from *Ark Royal*, the catapult bridle well in evidence. For obvious reasons, the catapult hooks were moved from the fuselage to the wing for the Gannet Mk 3.

COURTESY PHILLP JARRETT

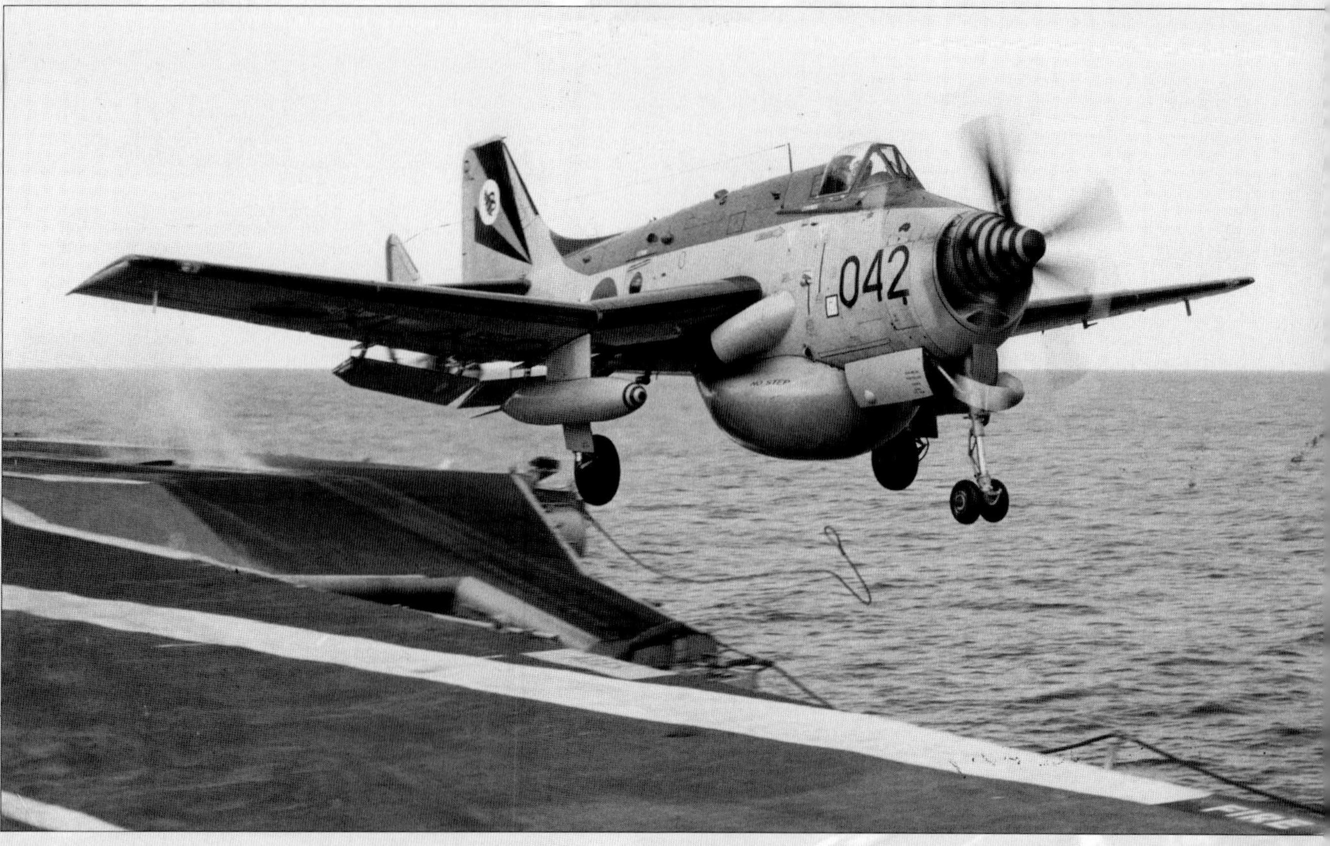

COURTESY PHILIP JARRETT

place by one or two precisely machined steel rings that slid down over the cylinder to keep it closed. The steel rings varied according to aircraft type, so as to give different break-out tensions as they snapped when the catapult reached the required pressure for that type. On the Gannet Mk 3, the holdback point was immediately behind the radome, and fixed to the same keel spar as the hook. On earlier marks, the holdback attachment point was at the bottom of the nose oleo.

Once centrally positioned, the shuttle of the catapult would be brought back and slid under the nose wheel. The bridle could then be attached. This was a twelve-foot length of steel wire cable with a spliced eye at each end. The eye ends fitted over two hooks stationed on the wings, outboard of the jet exhaust stubs, on the A.E.W. Mk 3, and on the fuselage, just ahead of the mainplanes, for the other marks. With two flight deck handlers holding the bridle in place, tension could be applied by moving the catapult hook forward to take up the slack. The Gannet then remained with all three wheels firmly on the deck to give a level launch attitude (unlike some of the contemporary jets, which were tensioned with the nose wheel clear of the deck).

Assuming all went well, the sequence was as follows. The handling crew confirmed that the bridle was on and tight, the Flight Deck Officer (FDO) indicated to the pilot that he should apply full power by rotating a green flag above his head, and a 'checks board' was held up which read, 'Brakes Off—Flaps Set—Full Power'. When the pilot was satisfied all was ready (about twenty seconds after arriving on the catapult in a worked-up ship), he would give a 'thumbs up' or a quick salute and the FDO would look ahead, judge the pitch of the ship and then drop the flag to knee height. The pilot would wedge his right elbow into his waist to ensure that inertia did not make him pull back on the stick, the catapult operator would hit the 'Fire' button and, after a pause of two seconds, the catapult was activated. The holdback snapped and the aircraft accelerated to flying speed and was airborne. The launch bridle was lost until, in later years, a 'bridle catcher' was introduced, protruding from the bow at flight-deck level. Unfortunately, the force with which the bridle was stopped was such that several strands of the wire were usually broken and it would have to be consigned to scrap anyway.

It sounds a simple procedure, but things did go wrong. One instance was in 1956 when XA401, a Mk 1 from 812 Squadron on board HMS *Bulwark*, slewed to port as it moved off and fell awkwardly over the port side of the ship. Happily, the crew escaped. Another was in July 1957 on board HMS *Bulwark* when she was moored at Sydenham, Belfast. There was a requirement for a compassionate flight to take a rating back to RNAS Ford and Lieutenant

Gordon Steer of 820 Squadron was selected to take him in a Gannet. There would be a catapult take-off as the ship had no forward speed. The pilot had no experience of this, and when the holdback broke prematurely, the pilot thought that the catapult—a hydraulic system—was merely a little slow, but XA390, with full power on both engines, motored over the bow of the ship. The pilot and his passenger were rescued, and although the aircraft was salvaged it never flew again.

In June 1956 the bridle fell off the launch hooks of 815 Squadron's A.S.1 XA354 on board HMS *Bulwark* and the aircraft, with power on, just rolled forward and fell off the front of the flight deck. The pilot, flying on his own, was saved by the planeguard helicopter. The same thing happened to an A.E.W. Mk 3, XL478, launching from HMS *Eagle*: despite the pilot braking and cutting the engines, it went over the bows, and the planeguard helicopter picked up the three crewmen.

One of the problems with the nose leg and nosewheel assemblies was a tendency for the bottom section of the oleo, with the wheels, to detach as the leg extended sharply when the aircraft left the deck. There was also at least one case of the lower portion of the nose leg falling off when the undercarriage was lowered for landing. All of these resulted in aircraft either diverting ashore or being held off until all others had landed so that they could take the barrier without blocking the deck and delaying subsequent landings. In every case there was considerable damage to the forward part of the airframe as the wheel-less oleo stub dug into the runway or deck.

While all marks of the Gannet were docile when handled normally, the aircraft did tend to bite when something out of the ordinary was being tried. Such mild exercises as a practice single engine landing or a flapless landing—both of which had to be thoroughly rehearsed in case of single-engine or hydraulic failure—could lead to people getting into all sorts of difficulties, some of which, sadly, culminated in fatalities. The Pilot's Notes for all marks did actually state that 'there may be a slight elevator buffet just before the stall with flaps up, but this should not be

Opposite: Gannet A.E.W.3 XL450 is launched from HMS *Ark Royal*. Catapult bridles were considered to be expendable—at least, up until the time of *Ark Royal*'s final refit, when special projecting catchers were installed. That for the waist catapult can be glimpsed in this photograph, although in this instance it appears not to be following the script.

Below: Another catapult-assisted A.E.W.3 take-off from *Ark Royal*, showing the aircraft's flaps at the fully down (40-degree) setting. Field take-offs generally required the use of 20 degrees of flap or of none at all: in this way, the aircraft was brought to flying speed as quickly as possible, thereby offering the pilot a greater safety margin should one of the engines fail.

COURTESY PHILIP JARRETT

VIA AUTHOR

COURTESY GEOFF WAKEHAM

COURTESY GEOFF WAKEHAM

relied on as a stall warning. There is no warning of the stall with flaps down.' There was an early consideration to have spoilers fitted on the inboard wings to ensure that any stall began there instead of at the wing tip, hence offering some buffet warning, but this modification was never incorporated.

With both engines running normally, the aircraft was responsive to the controls and would climb, dive, roll and yaw to order. It was not cleared for aerobatic manœuvres, however, and it had a low 'g' limitation (about 3.5), which was required for recovery from a weapon-delivery dive. Moreover, the engines had no means of oil and fuel supply when under negative 'g'. Nevertheless, some bold aviators—curiously, also old aviators; the two do not always go together—have told me in confidence that at least one pilot performed a barrel roll, and another looped an A.S.4 (without the wing tips falling off). Both manœuvres could be, and should have been, carried out with positive 'g' applied at all times.

The flying controls were all manually operated, with no hydraulic assistance. Aerodynamic loads were kept low by means of spring tabs on ailerons, rudder and elevator. With no air load (that is, when the aircraft was on the ground) the control and tab moved as one; when airborne, if the aircraft was to turn left, the stick moved to the left would move the starboard spring tab up and the force created would move the aileron down—and *vice versa* for the port aileron. The elevator and rudder worked in the same way. The starboard aileron, one elevator and the rudder each had a trim tab as well to eliminate in-flight loads. The aileron trim was electrically activated, whereas the rudder and elevator were moved mechanically by means of trim wheels in the cockpit.

Because of the long endurance, the aircraft was fitted with an autopilot, which, although unrefined, did at least enable hands-off flight while the aircraft maintained (barometric) height, speed and direction. It actually selected attitude rather than speed and assumed that the pilot would have the aircraft trimmed for level flight at a desired power setting, whereupon it then maintained attitude rather than speed *per se*. When in operation it used its own hydraulic supply to power small servo units on ailerons, elevators and rudder. These had limited authority, but did ease the load on the pilot. Each axis had a limit cut-out switch, and the autopilot had to be selected 'off' for landing.

The autopilot for the AEW version was a later mark of the original fitted to the A.S.1s and 4s, which had not only the basic axis locks and limit switches but also cut-outs that operated should the aircraft roll, yaw or pitch at greater than a given rate. These worked well, but the initial setting-up required the observer to unstrap himself and turn round in the after cockpit to reach the bank of potentiometers and permit him to carry out fine tuning. All the while, the pilot was imposing the different manœuvres to cause the pitch and roll cut-outs to operate. Such an operation always involved a busy half-hour.

The A.S.1s and 4s had a hydraulic system, which, should it fail, could lead to a situation where neither undercarriage nor flaps could be lowered. The lack of an undercarriage was serious, especially when embarked, when it invariably resulted in a landing into the barrier. This latter consisted of a upper and a lower wire with vertical nylon straps between the two. It was rigged between two strong stanchions mounted either side of the flight deck, and the disabled aircraft would make a shallow, hook-down approach into it, the nylon stretching as the bands wrapped around the mainplanes. The result was a moderately damaged aircraft with an engine that had been shock-loaded as the propellers hit the deck turning at flying speed. The aircraft would have to be disembarked to a repair yard for a six-month rebuild.

Flapless landings were practised to cater for the occasion when, with the undercarriage down, hydraulic failure prevented the flaps from lowering. The flaps were of the Fairey Youngman type, such that, as they lowered, they dropped backwards and below the wing, thereby increasing the effective wing area and providing a 'slot' beneath the wing which gave better airflow (and in the Mk 3 also permitted a measure of jet efflux to pass through as well). A flap failure on its own was not serious and would merely result in a flatter than usual approach at a slightly higher speed. Pilots had to remember that without flap the stalling speed was increased by 10 knots. The Pilot's Notes commented that 'the stall has very little natural warning and must be approached with caution'. This tendency to stall would be exacerbated in a turn using over 30 degrees of bank and was

Opposite: On 29 July 1959 the undercarriage of 814 Squadron's Gannet XA645, flown by Lieutenant J. Gunning and with Lieutenant Noel Unsworth as observer, failed to function as the aircraft was preparing to land on board HMS *Centaur*, and this was the result. The safety barrier was raised, but, being of the latest nylon type designed primarily to stop runaway jet aircraft, it did not take kindly to the eight whirring blades of the Gannet and, as can be seen here, was somewhat shredded on impact. Interestingly, the aircraft appears to have two live rocket projectiles (RPs)s beneath the starboard wing.

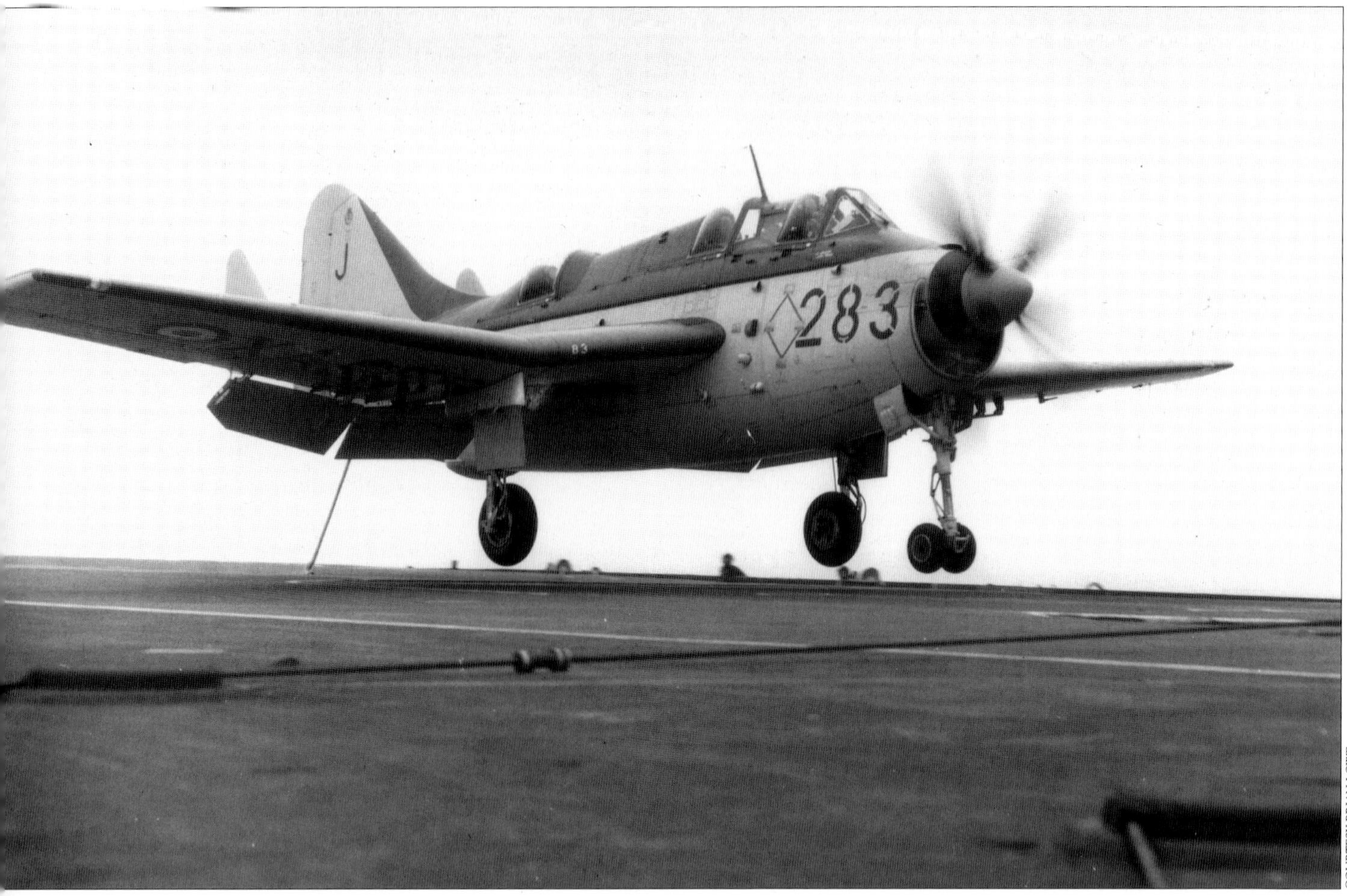
COURTESY BRIAN LOWE

particularly hazardous if flying on only one engine. One such occurrence was in 1972 during a Staff College demonstration at Yeovilton. Then, while on one engine and flapless, a Gannet stalled in a fairly tight turn and crashed. Sadly, all the crew members were lost.

A very early production aircraft was nearly in trouble at Lee-on-Solent in 1953. As related by Lieutenant Dan Carter, who witnessed the incident, 'Slim' Sear, demonstrating the then new Gannet at the Lee Air Day prior to the Coronation Flypast, was flying slowly on one engine, with undercarriage and flaps down. There was a problem when he tried to relight the other engine and, very close to the ground, he only just managed to do so. An accident would have been particularly embarrassing as the Coronation Flypast was to be the Gannet's first major public showing.

I remember the Lossiemouth Air Day in 1963, when a Gannet Mk 3, XP226, whilst displaying its prowess in stopping and restarting engines while airborne, was unable to relight the port engine when in a low and tight turn. The pilot lost speed and stalled at low level, belly-landing on the runway and shedding propeller tips, drop tanks and of course the radome. There was a royal spectator, who, together

Above: An inch-perfect carrier landing by the pilot of Gannet A.S.4 XA456 of 814 Squadron on *Eagle* in 1957 or 1958.
Right, upper: XA454, an A.S.4 converted to a carrier onboard delivery (COD) vehicle, demonstrates the Gannet's approach attitude as it crosses *Ark Royal*'s round-down.
Right, lower: The result of an overshoot at White Waltham involving WN455, an A.S. Mk 1 flown by Lieutenant M. K. L. Whitwam, who had been obliged to land in a severe rainstorm.

with a group of classmates from nearby Gordonstoun School, might have witnessed this—had he and his companions not been heavily engaged in the food tent at the time!

As a precaution against oil-pressure failure, and hence allowing the propeller to move under centrifugal force to the fully fine position of 6 degrees, a Flight Fine Pitch Stop was introduced in the 101 engine, which was activated when the undercarriage was raised or lowered. Thus after take-off, with the undercarriage raised, the stop was inserted so that, in the event of a loss of power to the engine (or oil pressure failure), the propeller would move only to the fine stop position of 21 degrees (in the A.S.1 and 4; 19 degrees in the A.E.W.3). Conversely, when the aircraft was approaching to land, as the undercarriage was lowered the stop was withdrawn and nothing was apparent until after landing, when the engines were throttled back as the constant

COURTEST GEOFF WAKEHAM

VIA AUTHOR

COURTESY BRIAN LOWE

speed was no longer required. This meant that constant speed was maintained throughout the landing approach, thereby giving very rapid response to the throttle being fully opened for a missed approach.

Main image: XP226 comes to grief at the Lossiemouth Air Day, 13 July 1963, its port engine having failed to re-light while the aircraft was making a tight turn.
Above: The aftermath of the incident. The aircrew were uninjured. XP226 was rebuilt and flew for several years. It now resides at the Newark Air Museum.

The problem for aircrews was that, in the landing configuration (that is, with the flight fine pitch stops withdrawn), should one engine lose power the propeller would move to the fully fine position and present an almost solid 'disc' to the airflow through the other propeller. This would also seriously disturb the airflow over the tailplane. This effect was similar to that produced when applying the air brakes on a jet aircraft, and would give a violent deceleration and nose-down pitch change. There was no recovery

action from this position, unless the aircraft had height to spare. Did this happen to some aircraft which mysteriously plunged into the sea? There were a number of occasions when this was almost certainly the cause of a Gannet loss. One such occurrence was in the Mediterranean in 1956 when an aircraft from 812 Squadron operating from *Eagle* was lost on final approach to the carrier; happily, the crew were picked up uninjured. The aircraft, of course, disappeared for ever, so no proper analysis could be carried out. Another possible occurrence of this phenomenon took place in November 1960 when XL495, a Mk 3 on transit from Hal Far to *Victorious*, suddenly dived into the sea. The pilot, Sub-Lieutenant Collins, bailed out but was killed, and the cause of the accident remained unresolved. Lieutenant D. S. McIntyre, a good friend of mine, was also the victim of a probable 'disc' occurrence over St Bride's Bay while on final approach during a night-time GCA to RNAS Brawdy in late 1964 with his instructor, Lieutenant Danny Ferguson, in T. Mk 5 Gannet trainer XG881. Yet again there was very little time for any radio message describing the nature of the problem. However, when the wreck was recovered it was found that the position of the propeller blades indicated that 'disc-ing' had almost certainly been the cause.

A problem that manifested itself only on the Mk 3 was associated with build standard of the engine. Paul Greenwood recalls that in 1962 HMS *Ark Royal* lost two aircraft in quick succession together with their crews. The fault was discovered only when it happened again just before the launch. An A.E.W.3 was on the catapult, running up to full power, when a bang was heard and the front propeller moved forward a few inches. Now disconnected from all pitch control, it went, under centrifugal force to 'superfine' pitch and continued to run at flying speed. Had this occurred during flight, the effect would have been to increase drag dramatically and to cut off the airflow to the tail, thus converting the aircraft into a brick—as was witnessed by the RFA which saw one of the previous crashes. He and his crew were told that, owing to some error in machining the inner propeller shaft, the latter had developed a stress fracture. Normally, Double Mamba Mk 102s were 'lifed' at 300 units per power engine. Until all engines had been checked and repairs and modifications had been carried out, the starboard engine was limited to 150 units only. Since many of the power units were at that time up to 100 units or more, the use of the starboard engine became very limited. Ashore, therefore, crews would taxy out on the port engine, start up the second engine at the marshalling point, take off, up wheels as soon as possible, check that the pitch stops had engaged and then shut down the starboard engine. The Royal Navy practice of referring to engines as

COURTESY BRIAN LOWE

'port' and 'starboard' obviated the risk associated with one member of the crew asking another, 'Have you shut down the right engine?'

Maintaining long patrols for either anti-submarine or AEW tasks did require the crew to conserve fuel in order to give them maximum time on task. For this the design of the Gannet was ideal, as it would fly on one engine perfectly happily once airborne. Flying for endurance on one engine did, however,

Above: A typical deck scene on board HMS *Victorious* in late 1960, with, aft, 849 Squadron 'B' Flight Gannet A.E.W.3s to port and 803 Squadron Scimitars to starboard. In the foreground can be seen three of the Palouste starters described on page 34 of this book.
Below: A Gannet A.E.W.3 utilising the emergency airfield arrester system at RNAS Brawdy.
Opposite: Gannet A.S.1 VR546—the first prototype—undergoing deck-landing trials on board HMS *Eagle* in 1952. With the introduction of the angled deck a few years later, the Deck Landing Control Officer ('batsman'), seen here at far right, would be redundant, replaced by the Landing Safety Officer positioned at the 'mirror'.

COURTESY DICK OINN

require changing them over every hour, so as to even out the hours consumed and maximise engine life. While the stopped engine would usually readily re-light as it was allowed to 'windmill up' in speed, there were a number of recorded occasions when it refused to do so. In unfeathering the stopped engine, and allowing it to windmill to self-sustaining speed, there was a drag penalty on the aircraft which caused its descent towards the sea or ground. With the early, 100-series engine, which had no pitch stop, full power on the good engine could not maintain level flight with the other windmilling in fine pitch; in contrast, with the 101 engine, running at 15,000rpm and with the pitch stop engaged, level flight was possible while the problem was sorted out by feathering the 'bad' propeller.

One incident of this nature was experienced by Lieutenant (O) Eric Coop in an A.S.1 aircraft in August 1956. Flying WN368 (813 Squadron, HMS *Eagle*), he experienced a power loss on the running engine and was obliged to carry out a single-engine landing at RNAS Hal Far. The principal concern of the crew had been to try to hand over the surface plot to another Gannet as they were descending towards the sea while the pilot struggled to start the other engine.

A further problem that might occur was 'strobing', in which one propeller lost its constant speed and the visual effect on the pilot was that of a strobe rotating at several rpm (depending on the mismatch between engines). There was a 'nudge' facility whereby the starboard engine speed could be varied

COURTESY JOHN BEWICK

COURTESY ERIC COOP

COURTESY ERIC COOP

slightly up or down to achieve synchronised speeds, but sometimes this was not sufficient.

The through-life problems with the engines of all marks of Gannet did mean that pilots had to practice single-engine failures. As has been seen, it was normal practice to fly on one engine, changing them over every hour, so there were plenty of opportunities for one to fail to re-light. A single-engine recovery to an airfield posed no problem at all—so long as it was a full-stop landing. Overshooting, or doing a 'touch and go', on one engine was slightly fraught as sometimes the good engine failed to achieve full power when demanded; similarly, if the pilot was slow in raising the undercarriage and flaps, the aircraft would be slow to accelerate. An early instance of this was in 1955 when A.S.1 XA509 of 737 Squadron from Eglinton was carrying out a practice single-engine overshoot at RAF Ballykelly, failed to achieve full power and sank down to make a wheels up belly-landing on the grass. Such ignominy at an RAF establishment!

More dramatic problems with the Double Mamba included several instances of engines merely failing in flight, as happened to XG832, an A.S.4, in December 1963 while on a night GCA into RAF St Mawgan. Fortunately, the crew managed to bail out and were rescued. Another instance involved A.S.1 WN457, on HMAS *Melbourne*: the Gannet's engine exploded on launch and the aircraft crashed into the sea.

With the Gannet's co-axial propeller arrangement there was, as had been remarked, no torque effect as with a single propeller, nor were there the asymmetric problems associated with aircraft with two wing-mounted engines such as the Mosquito and Meteor. For these types there was a 'critical approach speed' below which it was not possible to keep straight, especially if full power had to be applied to the live engine, as there was insufficient rudder control to overcome the yawing force. Thus, without this limitation, single-engine approaches were perfectly possible, keeping in mind the care needed with the flaps and in turns.

There appear to have been a number of recurring problems afflicting the earliest Gannets from 1953, and, despite a number of manufacturer's modifications, these remained troublesome until the Gannet went out of service in 1978. Between them, these problems resulted in some 50 to 60 aircraft being written off, sometimes with the loss of their crews, out of a production total of nearly 380; 22 of the 44 AEW aircraft finally built were affected in this way. The problems centred around the undercarriage (especially the nose assembly), the wing-fold mechanism, the engines and the hydraulics. The first three of these are covered elsewhere in this book.

The Gannet had only relatively low-pressure hydraulics, running at between 2,100 and 2,600psi (the bigger jets ran at a nominal 4,000psi). Thus hydraulic leaks were not quite as serious in the Gannet, although in the early models, despite their having some emergency back-up in the form of accumulators and a hand pump, a number of aircraft did lose hydraulic pressure. This often resulted in the failure of the undercarriage to lower and could even lead to the bomb bay falling open, and the shortcoming was addressed by the addition of more non-return valves in the systems.

An example of this problem was demonstrated at RNAS Hal Far when a crew (who had better remain anonymous) took an A.S.1 up for a post-major-maintenance test-flight one Saturday morning. Everything seemed to be well in order and, from

Left: Hal Far, 13 August 1956: WN367 of 812 Squadron arrives in unconventional fashion following a hydraulic failure.

Main image: WE488, the third Gannet prototype, demonstrates single-engine flying with the radome lowered.

COURTESY PHILIP JARRETT

Above: 825 Squadron's A.S. Mk 1 XG790 on finals into Culdrose in 1957, its arrester hook not needed and hence retracted.
Opposite: Gannet A.E.W 3s of 849 Naval Air Squadron demonstrating the configuration for landing at sea. Over a decade separates the dates of these two photographs, during which period the Gannet's 'lumps and bumps' had changed in character in order to accommodate the type's various internal upgrades.

exuberance, the pilot offered his crew—an observer and one of the Squadron electrical officers—a few aerobatics, which were strictly forbidden in the Gannet. They successfully completed rolls and a loop or two, during the course of which a very loud *clunk* was heard. On return to the airfield, the Gannet had no hydraulic pressure, one of the accumulators having broken loose, and the result was that the undercarriage refused to lower. After an hour or so spent burning off fuel, the crew were cleared to land on the minor runway, and did so in a cloud of dust with very mangled propellers. Photographs of this incident appear on page 54.

The aircraft was a true all-weather operator and capable of flying in most conditions and, of course, at night. The cockpit illumination was adequate rather than wonderful, and it was always advisable to carry a torch. There was a selection of lights, with ultra-violet on the instrument panel, red floodlights for the side consoles, and an emergency white light from its own battery. Night flying from an airfield is always straightforward, but a carrier approach at night does require considerable concentration. The first obvious difference is that there is no ground lighting from nearby towns to give positional orientation. The other difference is that airfields have lights down both sides of the runway in use, which give adequate reference to enable the pilot make a visual circuit to the same pattern as that for a daytime landing.

Carriers do not have runway lights either side of the landing area. The deck is very short anyway, and the lights are only down the centreline. Thus the visual reference is totally different and there is no perspective to judge height and distance. Therefore the circuit, or controlled approach, must be flown to the correct pattern for height and speeds until on 'finals', when the mirror sight is visible to confirm the glide path. It is then necessary to keep a wary eye on the airspeed as turbulence from the funnel gases and from the deck itself can cause the unwelcome loss of a few knots at the wrong moment.

Finally, vision at night is difficult on the deck, and at various times trials have been conducted with both white and red floodlighting for the whole deck to try to give it more perspective. This, though, may have the undesirable side effect of spoiling a pilot's night vision.

Operating ashore, the Gannet's circuit was unremarkable, with undercarriage lowered downwind at 150 knots, followed by half flap (20 degrees) on the turn to 'finals' and full flap (40 degrees) at no more than 135 knots for the landing. The visual approach was controlled and steady, and

COURTESY PHILIP JARRETT

RICHARD L. WARD

the engines at approach power offered a rapid response to throttle movement, albeit with a slight delay if the throttles were slammed forward for full power (which was a more important factor when deck landing). Ailerons were responsive down to the landing. The threshold was crossed at 90–95 knots depending on wind, weight, etc. Care was taken to avoiding rapid throttle movement, and the thottle was never closed to ground idle below 100 knots until landing had been accomplished.

After touch-down, the nose wheels could be held off the ground for a while whilst the engines were throttled back and dropped below constant speed. Once the nose gear was in contact with the runway, equal pressure with both foot-operated wheel brakes brought the aircraft to a stop, although the nose

COURTESY BRIAN LOWE

Above: An 824 Squadron Gannet lands on board HMS *Albion* in early 1957. The twin nosewheels will touch the flight deck first, the long-stroke of the oleo absorbing the initial shock for a split second before the mainwheels touch down. Unusually, only the Flying Tel's canopy is open.
Opposite, top: A Gannet courier aircraft, having landed on *Hermes*, awaits the fitting of its nose-wheel steering arm.
Main image: XA456, an A.S. Mk 4 on the strength of 814 Squadron, lands on board HMS *Eagle* in 1958. Following the standard safety procedure for landing at sea, all three cockpit canopies have been slid fully back.

wheel assembly was liable to 'shimmy' in a violent side-to-side oscillation, which could, potentially, cause structural damage. This had happened to the first prototype in November 1949, and it was still happening to the Mk 3 nearly thirty years later. An extreme demonstration occurred at RNAS Brawdy in September 1968 after Lieutenant-Commander Paul Stevenson landed, a violent shimmy causing the nose leg to collapse, in turn allowing the propellers to hit the runway and a fire to start. The aircraft, XL498 (a machine I had earlier force-landed after a double engine fire), was not subsequently repaired. This incident should not have occurred as there was a clutch mechanism to lock the wheels together over a speed of about 15 knots in order to avoid shimmy.

When it came to carrier landings, while the aircraft was essentially in the same configuration as that for a shore landing, a number of factors—turbulence from the ship's superstructure, the wind not blowing straight down the deck, difficulty on the part of the pilot in following the mirror landing sight—could, and did, cause difficulty. One obvious hazard was that the aircraft might not catch one of

COURTESY GEOFF WAKEHAM

COURTESY BRIAN LOWE

the arrester wires (of which there were generally four on offer). With an angled deck this was not a problem as there was an unobstructed overshoot path and so, with full power applied, the aircraft could safely 'go round' again. (It was always important to keep the engine revs at 15,000 until the hook had engaged, otherwise there could be insufficient 'acceleration time' to ensure that full power was achieved before passing the end of the flight deck!) The pilot was always informed, in case he did not realise he had missed all the wires, with the R/T call 'Bolter' On occasions, a hook damper malfunction could allow the hook to 'skip' over the wires with the same effect, as was the case in 1958 with A.S.1 XA421 (815 Squadron, *Ark Royal*), which ditched after missing the wires. The crew was saved. Another instance of this involved a Mk 3, XP224 from *Hermes*, in 1969 when, after the aircraft had missed the wires and the pilot had applied full power, flames were seen coming from the jetpipes (possibly as a result of a compressor stall) and the aircraft ditched. Again, the crew was rescued.

Because of the difficulties of escaping from a submerged or sinking aircraft, it was standard practice to have the canopies open for carrier take-offs and landings—except in the Mk 3. This is known to have helped several people get out who might otherwise have not escaped. It was noticeable, however, that the pilots of the Mk 3 always had greater problems than did the two observers, who had only to blow their hatches off to give an easy escape route. With the weight of the engines, the nose of the aircraft was bound to sink first. Paul Greenwood remembers that in 1962, on *Ark Royal*, the pilot of XP198 was lost after the hook broke during the landing run. After he entered the water, he operated the hood jettison, which disconnected the hood from the jack; thereafter, because the aircraft was nose-down, every time he pushed the hood back it rolled forward before he could wriggle through the gap. Tragically, he drowned. Later on, a catch was fitted to hold the hood open—although the resultant gap was still only sixteen inches.

Addressing these problems, in the final years of the Gannet's service an underwater escape assistance package was devised and installed. This worked on compressed air and first removed the canopy, then pushed the pilot, in his seat, clear of the aircraft, inflated his life jacket and finally separated him from the seat. It is not known

Below: XL451 landing on board HMS *Victorious* during the A.E.W.3's proving trials in mid-1959. The underwing drop tank appears to have been 'borrowed' from a Hawker Hunter.
Right, upper: An 849 Squadron 'B' Flight A.E.W.3 crosses HMS *Centaur*'s round-down, affording a view of the Gannet's stalky undercarriage and, *ergo*, very lengthy arrester hook.
Right: An apparent 'bolter' on board HMS *Eagle* by an 814 Squadron Gannet. The reason here is unknown.

COURTESY PHILIP JARRETT

COURTESY PHILIP JARRETT

COURTESY BRIAN LOWE

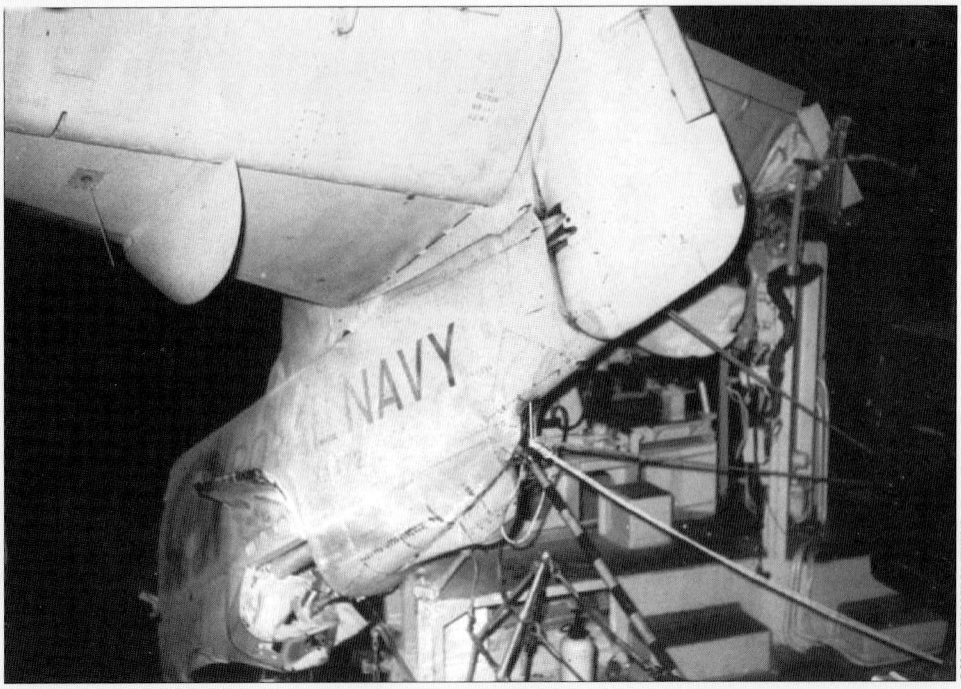

COURTESY JOHN BEWICK

Left: The remains of 831 Squadron's XA472, which on 4 September 1962 struck *Ark Royal*'s round-down on attempting to land and, as a result, was pitched overboard leaving the tail section wrapped around the projector sight. The author relates the story in the accompanying text.
Below: A Gannet folding its wings was always guaranteed to drop the jaws of the uninitiated, the concertina-like movement giving the impression from afar that some sort of horrible accident was taking place. WN346, 812 Squadron, HMS *Eagle*.
Opposite: Once the wings were permanently stowed, bracing struts were fitted to give additional rigidity.

whether the system was ever tried in anger, though the theory seems impeccable.

Other hazards of which pilots had to be aware included the possibility of mishandling close to stalling speed. In 1960 this caused XA472, an E.C.M. Mk 6, to hit the round-down of *Ark Royal*'s flight deck. The fuselage broke as it hit, and the aircraft slid along the deck. The front section then hit the port landing sight and fell over the ship's side, coming to rest inverted on the surface of the

COURTESY BRIAN LOWE

sea. The tail section aft of the rear cockpit remained wedged on the sight. The crew all managed to escape and found that a Carley float had been dislodged from the ship and was there for them to cling to while awaiting rescue. This arrived in the form of the frigate *Eastbourne* as planeguard, and the ship's sea-boat picked them all up in short time. The position was made slightly more hazardous by a crew member who fired his distress flares from the float while surrounded by a large area of kerosene. Luckily there were no dire consequences. The crew, including Lieutenants David Pickles and Tony Hayward, were returned to the carrier next day by jackstay transfer. The Projector Sight Officer during the incident, Lieutenant John Bewick, for his first and only time had recourse to the emergency escape chute from the sight to the safety net rigged below. Neither he nor the pilot were sure if the other was alive until they met the next day.

An 849 Squadron 'C' Flight aircraft, XL477, stalled on final approach to *Hermes* off Ceylon and the aircraft was seen to roll and crash. Two of the three crew escaped—though not the pilot, so the cause was unknown. Another accident associated with the danger of a engine failing on the approach—that is, with the flight fine pitch stops not engaged—involved another Mk 3, this time XL493, on the last stages of a night CCA. One engine failed, the propeller would not feather and the aircraft ditched. The crew was saved.

On completion of a safe landing ashore, it was usual for the Gannets to fold their wings so that they would occupy less parking space; afloat, of course, it was obligatory. The folding mechanism was complicated and a source of never-ending fascination for spectators. When a COD Gannet landed at the US Navy field at Subic Bay one day in 1960 and was taxying in after it had folded, the Control Tower asked the crew to repeat the procedure as more people had arrived to witness the sight! Again, at RNAS Lossiemouth one day in the early 1960s, a COD Gannet had called in for mail and happened to be followed along the taxiway by a US Air Force Convair F-102 Delta Dagger visiting from the US base at Keflavik in Iceland. The American pilot was so fascinated by the sight of the Gannet crumpling its wings that his aircraft ran off on to the grass and had to be pulled out by a tractor!

COURTESY BRIAN LOWE

WEAPONS, STORES, CAPABILITIES

Commander Simon Askins

THE two distinct rôles required of the Gannet—first, anti-submarine warfare and, in the aircraft's reincarnation, airborne early warning—meant that the two principal variants had totally different capabilities. Marks other than the AEW version could carry a very useful selection of weapons.

The Gannet A.S.1 and 4 carried a similar armament and may be considered together; moreover, most of what they could do could also be demonstrated or practised in the T.2 and T.5 trainers as these had bomb bays that could accommodate identical loads. The anti-submarine versions of the aircraft were developed in the era when submarines were located by spotting conning towers or even the 'snorkels' by radar from afar and then speeding towards a target to attack it before it dived too deep. All the marks carried sonobuoys and marine markers (smoke floats), the latter as a reference point (which lasted about an hour) from which to work. They were carried in the bomb bay doors and could be released by the pilot, one at a time as required. Early aircraft also had a rotary dispenser which could be carried underwing instead of a drop tank, freeing up space in the bomb bay for further armament to be carried there.

The radar, ASV-19B (ARI.5838), was a development of the original airborne set used in Swordfish aircraft during World War II. It was controlled by the operator in the rear cockpit and had an 'A'-scope presentation. This was frequently sufficient to alert the crew to a possible submarine up to ten miles away and allow them to position for an attack run.

The precise location of a submerged submarine was calculated by the observer by dropping sonobuoys—usually three or four at a time but as many as twelve in a pattern. The early sonobuoys were non-directional and, once dropped (each with its own parachute), raised an aerial and lowered a hydrophone. The received signal from each buoy gave a volume of noise—most of it caused by propeller cavitation—and by comparative volume a rough position for the submarine could be estimated. Later types of sonobuoys were directional: once in the

COURTESY BRIAN LOWE

Opposite: XA420 of 824 Squadron about to depart on a free take-off from HMS *Bulwark* with an underwing load of rocket projectiles. By this time, 1957, the days of the individual RP were numbered, their place on the RN inventory eventually being taken by podded rockets.
Right: The underwing Saunders-Roe rotary dispenser that equipped Gannet A/S variants could accept six T.1945 omni-directional sonobuoys (but not T.1946 directional sonobuoys). The bomb bay could accept either, along with various combinations of bombs, practice bombs, flares, mines and/ or a torpedo. Flares and markers (smoke floats) could be accommodated also in the bomb bay doors, while smoke floats could also be dispensed separately via a chute.

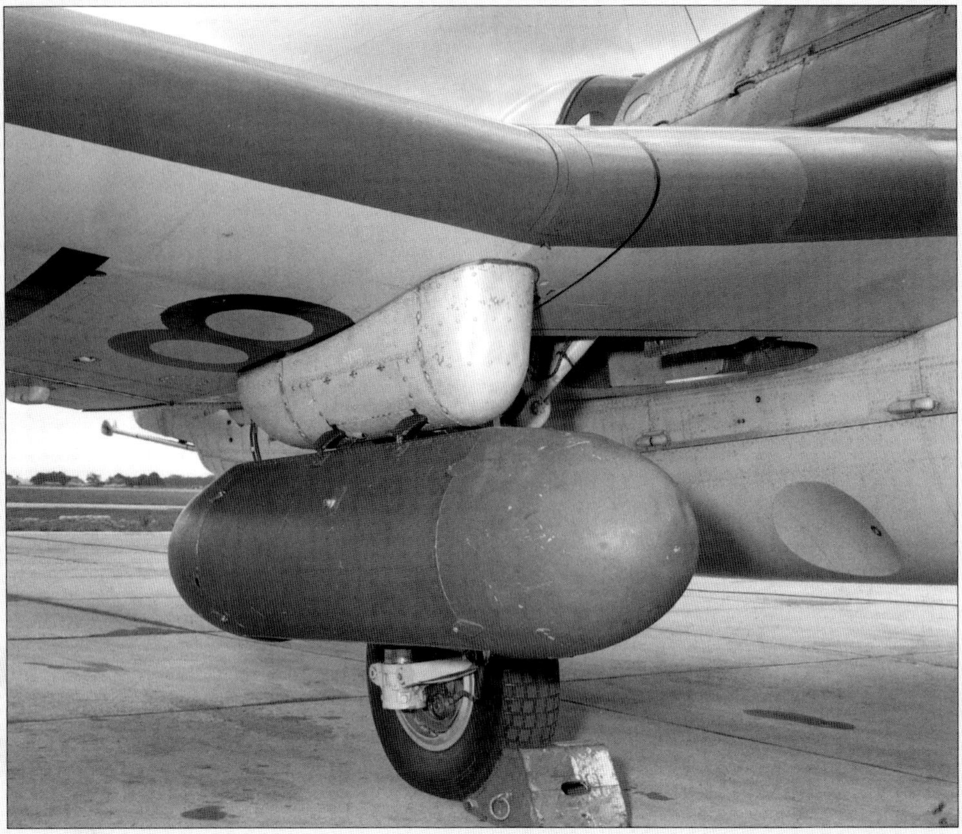

COURTESY PHILIP JARRETT

water, the hydrophone rotated and could transmit an approximate bearing of the noise received. This was analysed on a dedicated sonobuoy 'A'-scope screen which was then manually plotted on to a chartboard, the position calculated, and a course-to-steer passed to the pilot.

The weapons used for the attack were conventional and many had seen service during the war. These included the Mk 11 depth charge, up to six of which could be carried in the bomb bay and which could be dropped singly or in pairs at up to 250 knots, either from level flight or in a 30-degree dive. The attack line was from ahead or astern, about 10 degrees off the line of the submarine's course. This allowed a margin of longitudinal error whereas a lateral attack would risk the weapons falling short of, or beyond, the target.

Alternative bomb bay loads were up to four 500-pound bombs, for attacking a surface ship or a surfaced submarine. These were usually delivered in a 20-degree or 30-degree (maximum 50-degree) dive, entered into from about 3,000 feet (higher for a 50-degree dive), at a release speed of up to 300 knots and from a starting 'roll-in' position with the target approximately on the wing tip. Alternatively, the bay could carry one or two Mk 30 torpedoes, which could be dropped individually in level flight, usually about half a mile from the estimated position of a submarine, from a height of 300 feet and at a speed of up to 240 knots, and were homed acoustically towards the target (as illustrated on pages 118–119).

A rarely used capability was the carriage of two mines which could be laid in suitably deep water. These weighed about 1,000 pounds each and were dropped from low altitude (200–300 feet) in the position directed by the command. Most types of mine had parachutes to give a gentler landing in water. There was also a capability, presumably checked out at Boscombe Down, to carry and drop a 2,000-pound store, either a bomb or a mine. This would be installed in the bomb bay, and the mode of delivery would have been in level flight for a mine and by dive attack for the bomb. None is known to have been delivered in anger.

The final weapon type was the rocket projectile, up to sixteen of which could be carried under each wing. These RPs could be either the 25-pound or the 60-pound variety, fixed to a 3-inch rocket motor. They were intended for attacks on any suitable surface target, such as a ship or surfaced submarine, or a shore target. Flare rockets (Lepus flares) could also be fired from the level or from a gentle climb, in order to provide illumination during a night attack. The aircraft were fitted with gyro gun sights to allow aiming, particularly for the RPs. However, as this equipment was not especially reliable, pilots sometimes had to resort to a chinagraph cross marked on the windscreen! This extemporary device did give a point of reference for aiming, but it was inaccurate because of the parallax caused by the pilot moving his head from side to side—improved by closing one eye, but still not ideal! One such attack was made in the Yemen against insurgents in the mountains, where precision was perhaps not essential.

The attack profile for RPs was similar to that for bombing. The projectiles could be selected to fire in pairs, fours, sixes or eights, the approach again being made from about 3,000 feet from a starting 'roll in' position with the target on the wing tip. The dive angle was usually either 20 or 30 degrees but could be up to 60 degrees (from a starting altitude of 5,000), which gave a more accurate result although on the subsequent pull-out one pilot did manage to

RICHARD L WARD

RICHARD L WARD

detach both outboard wing sections. It appears that he hit the slipstream of the lead aircraft, which overstressed his own. The tips came off simultaneously and the pilot, Lieutenant Eric Taylor, in a great feat of airmanship, managed to land the aircraft. He carried out a GCA at RNAS Eglinton— which had a long straight run-in—from a turn so wide that he had to be cleared through Irish airspace, and controlled the heading and roll by use of his rudder. He was given a big pat on the back for this.

The A.E.W. Mk 3 was cleared to carry stores underwing only as it had no bomb bay. It could carry 100-gallon drop tanks, the Palouste starter, an Air–Sea Rescue (ASR) dinghy package ('G-dropper') and the Mks 43 and 44 torpedoes. The dinghy was for emergency rescue for other aircrew in the sea, and to assist this operation marine marker flares could also be dropped to help estimate wind speed before the dinghy pack was released. These were carried in a small stores bay located on the keel of the aircraft below the observer station. The use of torpedoes was considered for operations with anti-submarine helicopters, thereby transporting a greater weapon load to the target area, but this was more a theory than a real concept. The Torpedo Trials Unit, based at RNAS Culdrose, conducted carriage, dropping and jettisoning trials with these weapons in the mid-1960s.

Operational flying for the A.E.W Mk 3 was therefore limited to AEW barrier patrols, working either alone or with another Gannet. The aircraft carriers and aircraft-direction frigates had radar systems which integrated with those in the Gannets so that the surface picture as seen by the Gannet observer could be relayed back to a ship via the 'Bell Hop' link. A similar facility exists nowadays for the AEW Sea Kings of 849, 854 and 857 Squadrons. Having a flight of four aircraft embarked on a carrier meant that, so long as three were serviceable, two could be maintained on task for considerable periods by means of staggered launches and recoveries.

The radar set in the AEW Gannet was a ground-stabilised PPI (Plan Position Indicator) display, that is, it took out the movement of the parent aircraft to give a true presentation of the surface picture with all apparent speeds relative to the ground (or of course the sea). Thus it was quite capable of giving sufficient levels of accuracy to enable the observers to act as fighter-control officers and to vector loitering fighters on combat air patrol to intercept any incoming raid or threat. Both observers had the same display, so while one was vectoring a fighter the

Opposite page: A close view of typical Gannet Mk 3 underwing stores: (upper) the 'G' dropper ASR dinghy in the port pylon; (lower) a 100-gallon drop tank on the starboard pylon.
Right: By comparison with the A/S (and trainer) versions of the Gannet, the Mk 3 could tote little in the way of ordnance or stores—unsurprisingly, as it was not primarily an attack aircraft. There was no bomb bay, but external wing stations could accommodate auxiliary fuel tanks (upper photograph), the 'G-dropper' dinghy pack, baggage pods, etc., and, in theory, torpedoes. However, external stores carriage had an adverse effect on the underslung APS-20F radar, and for this reason Gannet AEWs would frequently patrol with only one wing station loaded (lower photograph).

RICHARD L. WARD

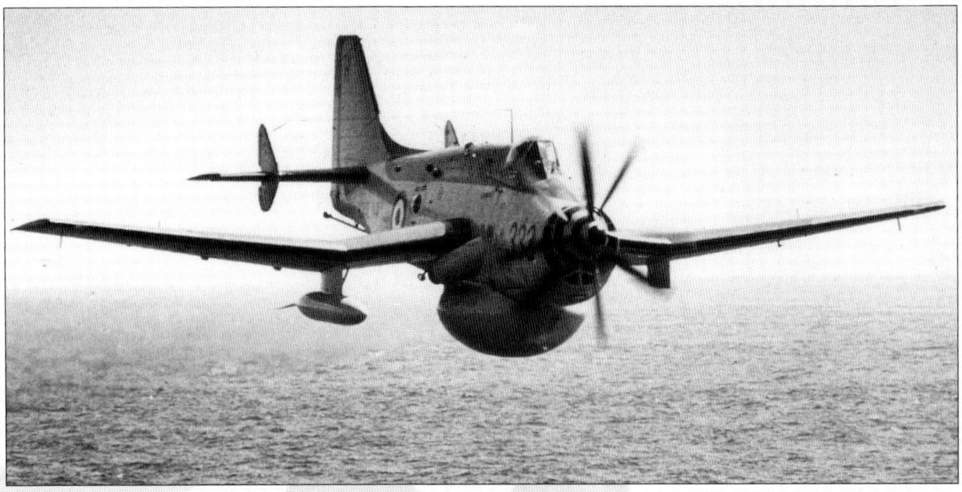
RICHARD L. WARD

other could maintain a watch on the whole area picture in case a further threat developed. The aircraft would operate at altitudes from 2,000 feet up to 15,000 feet, the radius covered by the radar increasing accordingly from 60 miles at low level to 200 miles at altitude.

The separation of the pilot from his observers in the rear cockpit of the Mk 3 did give rise to interesting situations. For example, in the event of a system emergency the alarm bells would sound in both cockpits but the indication of the type of emergency would show only on the pilot's Central Warning Panel, requiring him to get the word to his crew. Lieutenant-Commander Alan Kennedy recalls two incidents when he was an observer in 'B' Flight embarked in *Victorious*. In one, he and his colleagues had manned aircraft while the ship was carrying out gunnery practice. The noise was deafening, even in the cockpit with doors closed and above the din of the aircraft's engines starting up. He and the second observer, Lieutenant Le Dieu, were carrying out their preliminary take-off checks when there was a further bang that sounded like the ship's gun but was followed by the alarm and the engine running down. There was no word from their pilot Lieutenant Allard, and all went quiet. After a few seconds Alan opened the rear door and called to the ground crew to find out if they were preparing to start up again. The question was met by much laughter and they were beckoned to come and see. The reason for the mirth was soon apparent: there had been a catastrophic failure. The front propeller was two feet clear of the rear propeller and the pilot was standing alongside clearly a little shaken. Bearing in mind their fate had the incident happened a few minutes later, on take-off, the question 'Why didn't you tell us?' seemed irrelevant.

The second incident arose when Alan was flying with a ferry pilot. The alarm bells rang and the pilot, in a heightened voice, called that a wing-fold warning light had come. Alan, trying to give some reassurance, retorted, 'Oh, it's probably a microswitch problem' and added, 'Keep a good watch on the wings . . . and should the wing-fold indicators pop up don't bother to tell me because I will be gone!'

With drop tanks carried, the AEW Gannet's endurance—particularly employing single-engine flying—could be extended to five hours. The limiting factor became the aircrew: the pilot had to fly the aircraft for the entire sortie, albeit with some assistance from the autopilot, while the two observers in the back seats, looking at radar screens for that length of time, tended to lose concentration. In practice, however, the carriage of a pair of drop tanks tended to obscure part of the radar transmission, so just one tank was frequently carried in order to keep the other side clear of obstruction.

* * *

As every commander from before Nelson's day has known, the need to be able to communicate with units away from the main base is paramount. While early naval aviators solved this problem by carrying a pair of carrier pigeons, this did limit to two the number of messages that could be sent back. The range was also limited, although a good pigeon could probably manage a greater range than could the early aeroplanes.

The advent of radio in aircraft during World War I offered a huge step forward—non-secure, of course, as a broadcast could be heard by anyone. Nevertheless, it did (and does) provide an essential element of both navigation and communication for aircraft operating away from a land base or from a ship.

It had always been appreciated that, in order to obtain the longest ranges—to several hundred miles—the lower radio frequencies are better at following the curvature of the earth while the very high frequencies, less prone to interference, are best for close range (line-of-sight) speech transmissions. Thus, for an aircraft designed to roam the skies seeking hidden threats, a range of different radios was essential to cover all possibilities.

As it was developed, additional avionics kit was made available and fitted in Gannets either in service—at the Naval Avionic Trials Installation Unit (NATIU) at Lee-on-Solent or at an RNAY such as that at Fleetlands and Donibristle—or by the manufacturer. These included the Doppler navigational unit called 'Blue Silk' by the services, and the electronic homers called 'Green Salad' and 'Violet Picture'. Aircraft carried UHF and VHF radios, plus HF for long-range communications—and LF for talking to submarines. A TACAN homer and IFF were also fitted to later aircraft. The ECM aircraft had several wide-band and narrow-band jammers. Once the equipment had been installed, the first aircraft again had to be cleared by Boscombe Down.

The Gannet Mk 1s and 4s carried VHF radios for communicating for 100 miles or so. This set was one of the TR.1934/36 range (ARI.5489/91). In addition to the radio, there was also an intercom amplifier to allow the observers to converse without using the radio side tone, thus leaving the pilot in peace. 'Green Salad', working through the main VHF set, gave the pilot a left/right indication on an instrument to show the relative bearing of another transmitting source, be it aircraft, ship or airfield. Because of the limited range of VHF transmissions, there was also a 'relay' set (ARI.5491), which worked on the same twenty set frequencies, receiving on one frequency and simultaneously re-transmitting the message on another. The VHF aerials were short (one- foot) whips mounted one on top of the fuselage ahead of the rear cockpit and another under the port wing tip.

By 1958 the new higher-frequency UHF radios had come into service and replaced the VHF systems. All marks of the Gannet from the Mk 4 onwards – including the A.E.W. Mk 3, carried two ARC.52 (ARI.18124) sets. These provided the same facilities as did the earlier sets, including the updated 'Violet Picture' homer, which again had a left/right indicator on the main instrument panel. The aerials changed from whips to blades, shorter, aerodynamically shaped and about three inches in width. The relay facility was maintained. A small emergency UHF radio with just the 'guard' channel (243Mcs) and one alternate channel was fitted on some aircraft in order to prevent a total loss of radio contact.

For longer-range communication, HF/MF sets (ARI.5206) were fitted in the Mk 1 onward, enabling speech to be transmitted literally thousands of miles: it was not unknown for an aircraft operating from a carrier in the Far East to call up its base in Britain to enquire about the weather or the latest cricket score. There was also a Morse key, which could be used for sending coded letter or figure groups for a classified message. In some atmospheric conditions Morse was easier to send and receive than voice. In the A.E.W. Mk 3, the final HF fit was a Collins single side-band set which had remarkably good capabilities. The HF sets were under the control of the observers in the rear cockpits. The only time a pilot was 'switched through' was if there was a particularly good programme or a significant news event on the BBC (long wave). The HF aerial for all marks of Gannet was a wire, rigged from a short mast in mid top fuselage back to the tailfin.

To try to avoid 'friendly fire' incidents, all the aircraft had IFF (Identification/Interrogation Friend or Foe). These were improved periodically as new sets became available and included ARI.5679 in the Gannet Mk 1, ARI.5848 in later A/S aircraft and

COURTESY RICHARD L. WARD

Above: A Gannet A.E.W.3 in service with the Gannet Support Unit, based at RNAS Lossiemouth, in late 1970. Part of the Gannet's complex of radio aerials is visible—UHF blade aerials on the upper starboard mainplane and on top of the fuselage, behind the pilot; HF wires strung from the mast behind the pilot to the top of the starboard finlet, then up to the top of the fin; and another HF wire aerial from the mast abaft the observer's position to the top of the port finlet. Other aerials, not visible here, are located beneath both the mainplanes and the tailplane.

ARI.23134 IFF/SSR in the A.E.W.3. This last had 10,000 settings for flight into controlled airspace as well as useful codes such as '7600', meaning 'I have lost my radio'. The aerials for these were smaller blade types, some being triangular in shape, and were mounted on the wing upper and lower surfaces.

In the early days Gannets had a ZBX homer. This receiver (ARI.5307) was tuned to the frequency of any of the master home airfields (or a particular aircraft carrier). The transmitted signal was in Morse code and the letter changed from 30-degree sector to 30-degree sector. For example, if receiving letter 'F', one knew one was on a bearing of between 030 degrees and 060 degrees from the source. It was crude, but helpful if there were no other aids, although it was quite difficult to interpret for a solo pilot flying on instruments and trying to navigate.

A somewhat better aid was TACAN (ARI.18107), which provided a true bearing and distance from the transmitter; again a particular frequency was allocated to airfields and carriers. This could also be switched to 'receive only' in times of radio silence and give bearing only (i.e., no range). However, in a conflict it would probably not be used by any station except possibly as a brief guide to returning aircraft.

Other kit fitted included the sonobuoy receiver (ARI.5487 or, later, ARI.18103), which enabled the observers to listen to the transmission from the sonobuoys which were in turn listening for submarine noise. A retractable whip aerial mounted on the port lower fuselage was designed for this equipment.

To provide radar stabilisation, the Mk 3 AEW aircraft had 'Blue Silk' (ARI.5885), which, once set up in flight, calculated aircraft speed and drift that, when combined with the output from the master compass, a G4MB, provided the signal to ground-stabilise the APS-20F search radar. This then gave the observers a true representation of the surrounding scene without the need to compensate for aircraft movement. A radio altimeter (ARI.5284) was also fitted, so as to provide a safe indication of the aircraft's true height above the sea. This had proved too unreliable to use on the anti-submarine versions of the Gannet but was better on the Mk 3 and enabled the pilot to fly 'blind' down to an altitude 100 feet if required.

Fenceposts and Maypoles

Lieutenant Dick Oinn

The function of the anti-submarine Gannets—that is, the Mks 1 and 4—was the detection and destruction of enemy submarines. The Gannet observer's task was pivotal to all operations, and for a typical sortie his duties might take the form of the following (with the caveat that the information offered here was applicable only to diesel-electric submersibles and was rendered obsolete after Exercise 'Rum Tub' in late 1957 and the revolution in submarine design that followed).

Using information given at the briefing regarding wind direction and speed, he would first lay a course to the designated search area. Periodically, or as dictated by changes in the observed weather conditions, he would find fresh wind applicable to the altitude of the search (which was usually fairly low). In order to do this he would drop a smoke float and the pilot would immediately turn the aircraft 180 degrees, fly on for two minutes and then turn another 180 in the same direction as the first turn. The pilot advised the side on which the float would be passed, the time of passing the 90-degree float position would be indicated, and then the time when float was 45 degrees astern. Armed with this information, the 'Soup Plate' calculator would indicate the present wind speed and direction.

Let us assume that the designated task is convoy protection. At the ordered distance ahead of convoy, the Gannet would then commence a 'creeping advance' search, probably sweeping at right angles to the track of the convoy track and adjusting for the speed of the ships. The observer would pass the courses to the pilot and, with his permission, lower the 'dustbin' and begin a search of the sea in a circular area around the aircraft to a radius of, as I remember, about 40 miles. There was a 'blind' area below the aircraft, and so the observer would need to keep a careful watch out of the window (which is all that 'non-Os' think he did, anyway!): it would be extremely embarrassing to have a snorkel the size of Blackpool Tower go by unseen because the observer's head was buried in the radar! What the observer was essentially searching for was a disappearing radar contact, or DRC. If a contact were not disappearing—in other words if there was one sweep and 'gone', followed by a dozen or so reappearing in about the same place—it would probably be a small boat or a piece of

Below: The lot of the Gannet A/S aircrews during the 1950s—scrutinising the wave-tops, both visually and electronically, for the slightest hint of an enemy conning tower, periscope or 'snorkel', more often than not with one engine shut down to conserve fuel and therefore extend the aircraft's range. Sea states were rarely this benign, however.

COURTESY BRIAN LOWE

COURTESY DICK OINN

Above: Dick Oinn of 812 Squadron glances from his observer's cockpit as WN369, a Gannet A.S.1, is seen on a sortie in company with another aircraft from HMS *Eagle*, 3 May 1956. With the phasing out of diesel-electric submarines in favour of nuclear-powered boats with their vastly increased underwater endurance, surface contacts became rarer and the A/S rôle had to change accordingly: the introduction of the A/S helicopter with its dipping sonar allowed for rapid repositioning in pursuit of a fast-moving target.

flotsam. A DRC, in contrast, could very easily be a snort or a periscope.

On receiving a 'threatening' contact, the observer calculated the course and distance to it, advising the pilot of the necessary changes of course the aircraft had to make in order to home on to it, and report, via the telegraphist (especially if at extreme range for R/T), to 'Ops' on board ship. En route to the contact point, a letter-coded 'Fence-post' non-directional sonobuoy would be selected for the initial search and the pilot advised accordingly (he, as I recall, had the control as to which letter-coded buoy was on which position on the selector). On arrival at the calculated last position of the DRC, the pilot was instructed to drop the smoke float and buoy, and at the same time the TAG was instructed to listen on the appropriate frequency on the sono-receiver, the observer doing likewise. If, as was usually the case, nothing conclusive was heard, a pattern of 'Fence-posts' and associated smoke floats, all with different frequency codes, would be laid. By this time a local area plot appropriate to the submerged speed of a quarry would have been set up, with the position of each sonobuoy marked.

If it were ascertained that a cavitating submarine was indeed in the search pattern, a 'Maypole' directional sonobuoy was selected. This could be received by both the observer and the TAG, both audibly and visibly on an 'A' scope, a horizontal display following the direction of the rotating beam of reception and shown as a trace of light that became stronger and brighter as the volume increased. As I remember, the beam followed from 020 to 340 from left to right, then from 340 to 020 as the cursor 'flew' back from right to left, a little higher on the screen. The centre of 'louder' gave the azimuth of the source of the sound (which one hoped was a cavitating propeller and not a crowd of shrimps—noisy little beasts!). A second 'Maypole', and eventually a progressing line of them, judiciously placed, gave the course and speed of the quarry, all appearing on the plot and with times carefully noted. All the information would constantly have been passed to 'Ops', who, it was hoped, would have been keeping things in progress at his end.

Further action would depend on circumstances. The submarine might have been totally unaware of the Gannet's presence: sonobuoys are entirely passive, and therefore should not have been detected, so that, even if the aircraft were carrying depth charges or homing torpedoes (or both), a 'kill' might be more likely to succeed if a frigate or other suitably armed warship could be dispatched, in which case co-operation with it might be preferable. That decision, however, was unlikely to be the aircraft's.

When it was time to go home, the course was passed to the pilot, including any modifications necessary owing to changes in the briefed course and speed of the carrier. The observer's plots were cleaned up (ensuring that any 'porkies' in the carefully maintained running narrative were not too obvious!) and the course and ETA of the aircraft, and of the carrier, were re-checked. The observer could then relax a little and sit back until touch-down, hoping that the driver had remembered how to park his cab.

Not Much of a View

Captain Mike Rawlinson OBE

The observer's view from the cockpit? Well, there wasn't much of one: the blister windows allowed very little scope! However, with the blinds closed, the radar flashed up and the aircraft flying at a couple of thousand feet or so, the view was expansive—out to the radar horizon, and at height, it was over an area of 125,000 square miles. As the 'Eyes of the Fleet', the AEW task provided plenty for the two 'lookers' to do.

The Gannet AEW observer's rôle may not have had the high profile of those flying in Buccaneer, Sea Vixen or Phantom squadrons, but with the combined operation of all these aircraft from carriers in the 1960s and 1970s, the time was acknowledged to represent the zenith of fixed-wing flying and professionalism in the FAA—and the observers, in *all* rôles, were playing their full part to make it so. It was a great time to be there—you could feel it!

And I was lucky. It was July 1962. I was sitting at my desk in London, when the phone rang:

'Mike, about your next job.'

Pause.

'We think you would do well in the Nav Div at A&AEE Boscombe Down. How does that sound?'

It sounded awful, and I told him so. I had previously served in two front-line Firefly squadrons and a Skyraider AEW flight from carriers in the Atlantic, the Med and the Far East and with the Helicopter Flight aboard HMS *Protector* in the Antarctic. This virtually continuous sea time was followed by appointments with the Observer School as the Navigation Instructor and two years with the Navigation Research & Development Department in the Ministry of Aviation. The latter posts were both professionally rewarding and enjoyable, but enough! I wanted to get back front line, and as the Appointer rang off I added, 'And I'm no boffin!'

Fortunately he took the point, and about a week later he rang again.

'Look, we need someone to go to 849 . . .'

'That's better'

'. . . to take over as CO of "A" Flight.'

'Great! When?'

'Well, right now!'

The next few weeks were hectic—a brief, promised holiday on the canals with the family; then to Culdrose to join 849 HQ for a shortened Gannet AEW conversion and get up to date on drills and the latest management and engineering procedures; and a call on the Captain, Captain Bartosik, who sped me on my way as only he could with 'And what makes you think you have the qualities to command a squadron?' After a final farewell and a dash to catch a hurriedly arranged flight to Lisbon, I joined HMS *Centaur* in Grand Harbour. Next day, at noon on 20 August, I felt that well-remembered punch in the back from the catapult shot and I was airborne again from an aircraft carrier. It was good to be back!

For the ex-AEW Skyraider observer, the advent of the Gannet AEW was good news. There was not a lot of difference in cockpit comforts or space for the larger chaps (and there seemed to be a lot of these), but in terms of equipment things were much improved. The enhanced detection ranges and clearer picture of the AN/APS-20F radar as displayed on an eight-inch screen in place of the three-inch was a major improvement. Electronic cursers with an automatic read-out of range and bearing replaced the archaic hand-plotting of contacts with a chinagraph pencil, and the radar antenna, now stabilised in azimuth and partially in the horizontal, ensured that the radar picture remained 'steady' during course and height alterations. An improved display of IFF responses (or was it SIF by then?), plus coded

RICHARD L WARD

Right: The port side of the Gannet A.E.W.3, showing the observers' hatch closed for flight. The normal operating/opening lever is centred beneath the circular window, and the 'diamond' is the the explosive door jettison warning. 'Step clear of consoles on entering', warns the notice immedately beneath the entry hatch.

RICHARD L. WARD

responses, greatly assisted in identification, while a comprehensive communication fit of 'diallable' radio frequencies provided easy multi-tasking with other units. Also changed was the attitude to AEW. From time to time in the early Skyraider days, there was scepticism by some about the capability of an airborne radar and the ability of the young observers, and that had now gone.

I well recall an incident just after joining 'A' Flight. A pair of Sea Vixens on a long-range, 'radio silent', hi-lo anti-ship sortie from *Centaur* had got a bit lost on their way back. An AEW Gannet observer on a different task happened to be monitoring their frequency and was surprised to hear the course they were given to steer to return to 'Mother'. 'Vixen Leader' sounded surprised too, and a few minutes later called for another; I guess TACAN was unavailable. The AEW observer became more concerned as the course given by the ship did not correlate at all with his radar picture. 'Leader''s voice now sounded agitated—the fuel gauges were probably dropping too fast for comfort. The AEW observer decided to broadcast.

'This is Anyface [i.e., AEW controller]. I hold unidentified contact in position *xyz*'.

As quick as a flash came the response from 'Vixen Leader': 'Roger Anyface. A steer for Mother, please!'

There was no hesitation: he went straight into the well-practised routine.

'Roger Leader squawk [i.e., turn on IFF]. Turn port ninety for positive ident'—followed immediately by 'Roger, hold you, steer *x* for Mother; *y* miles to run.'

There was relief in the voice and a well-deserved glass in the Wardroom that evening.

The Gannet AEW observer worked very hard to provide the very best. 'Paf' Grant recalls that if, on getting airborne, the radar appeared below par it was possible to 'tweak' it.

Left: The characteristic radome of the AEW version of the Gannet—little changed in appearance from that on the earlier AEW Skyraiders. With the disbandment of the Gannet squadrons, the kit passed to the Shackletons of No 8 Squadron RAF and was only finally phased out of service when the latter re-equipped with 'mushroom-topped' Sentry AEW aircraft—a quite remarkable example of longevity for a single system.

Right: The starboard side of an A.E.W.3, with the hatch open and the two observers seated. In front of them are the two PPI radar screens, above which are basic flight instruments—speed, height and compass. The 'blister' window has a blind to keep out the light.

RICHARD L. WARD

COURTESY DAVID HOBBS

Left: The interior of the AEW Gannet observers' cockpit, showing the two eight-inch PPIs—a big improvement on the minuscule display provided in the AEW Skyraider.

However, this required the dexterity of Houdini and, being in a heavy cumbersome immersion suit, the fitness of a gymnast. Having unstrapped his parachute, the observer then manœuvred in the cramped space to kneel on the seat, stretch his head and arms down to the cockpit floor, and then locate and open a small panel which gave access to the duplexer unit in the radome. Try it in the front seat of a car. While 'tweaking' with a screwdriver, the second observer gave an encouraging commentary (or otherwise) on improvements to the radar picture. The observer's humour in this undignified and uncomfortable posture was not helped by the exhaust fumes that wafted into his face. It was all a bit hazardous, and the more so if the pilot forgot what was going on in the rear cockpit and made an unannounced turn. But it was worth all the effort if it achieved better results.

Our pilots were heroes and had the patience of Job, being required to fly straight and level for hours on end to give the observer the steady platform for a good radar picture. But not always. Paul Orchard recalls that, having detected a group of 'enemy' ships during a Fleet exercise, his pilot, Richard Gregory, shouted, 'Great! I can see them too!' and, with that, put the aircraft into a dive.

'What hell are you doing?'

'Going to bomb them! What do you think?'

'Yes, but I've lost my picture! And what with?'

'I'm taking my boot off!'

Now fast approaching low over an RFA tanker, Pilot Gregory opened his cockpit and threw the said boot at the ship. Wondrously, it landed on the deck. I understand it was 'stuffed' and had pride of place in the Officers' Dining Room for a number of years thereafter!

Since 1952, in the Royal Navy, AEW and 849 Squadron have been synonymous. The Squadron is unique in being the only FAA unit in this rôle, and in this respect is self-assessing. Great credit is due, therefore, to the consecutive Senior Observers at Squadron HQ and Flight level, who pioneered the art form needed by the Fleet for effective airborne area surveillance, maximum detection ranges, and co-operation with other squadrons to ensure maximum success in their particular tasks when required. The deployment to sea of the AEW Gannets with their specialised observers was a major factor in enhancing the defence capability of the Fleet throughout this time and was lost only with the demise of the fixed-wing carriers in 1978. It was no surprise that it was the lack of AEW a few years later that caused major concerns during the Falklands War. It is encouraging to know that the Squadron is again back in commission.

Screwdriver a Necessity

Lieutenant Brian Grindley

How did the occupant of the rear cockpit of a Gannet A.S. Mk 1, facing aft and looking at an extremely large tailfin, come to be there? Very little, if anything, has been recorded concerning the rôle of Communications Ratings as the operators of the A/S equipment, whose tasks encompassed the operation of sonobuoys and of the aircraft's radar and HF communications. Even official and semi-official documents tend to gloss over the contribution that they made. I myself was for some time a 'Flying Tel', and so, if you will indulge me, I will try to rectify, in part, these omissions.

The aft cockpit of an anti-submarine Gannet was manned by a Communicator—a Telegraphist, whose title was later changed to Radio Operator. He was a member of the sub-branch in the Fleet Air Arm known as Leading Telegraphist (Flying), abbreviated to L/Tel (F), which was later retitled L/Tel (Air) and subsequently Leading Radio Operator (Aircrew), or LRO (Air). To ourselves, we were simply the Flying Tels.

In General Service, aboard ship, Communicators, in common with other branches, had separate messes. Telegraphists and Signalmen, being watchkeepers, always had their own mess deck, which was never shared with anyone else. The Flying Tels, though not watchkeepers, roughly followed that tradition, in that we did not live in, nor share, the same mess decks as the ground crews when on board. In HMS *Centaur*, half our number lived in the communications mess deck and the other half were given 'G' Ready Room to use as accommodation and for the safekeeping of flying clothing. We all used it as our crewroom during the day. In HMS *Eagle*, however, the movement of rating aircrew on to the ship caused quite a stir when it was realised that cabins for them had been incorporated into the build designs, the aircrew cabins having been appropriated by personnel such as the Master-at-Arms and other heads of department senior rates, who objected quite strongly to the thought of being moved so that leading rates aircrew could use them—or so I was led to believe.

Communicators were chosen to operate the sonobuoy receiving equipment required by an anti-submarine aircraft presumably for their ability to pick out, from extraneous noise, the sound for which they were listening, possibly a Morse or other form of signal, often very faint and perhaps from a great distance. They needed also to be able to operate High Frequency (HF) transmitting and receiving equipment. They were required to be Leading Rates or to have passed the professional course and be awaiting promotion. The volunteers undertook a selection procedure at RNAS Lee-on-Solent, which consisted principally of an interview at which their knowledge of the Fleet Air Arm and its aircraft was assessed, together with their general suitability. This was followed by an Air Medical at the Central Air Medical Board just down the road. There they were examined for fitness, and, strangely, the length of their thighs, which were measured in case there was ever a necessity to eject from a jet aircraft in which they might be flying. They had eyesight examinations, which included a night visual acuity test after a period of dark adaptation. Prospective aircrew were further tested for colour perception.

On their original entry into the Royal Navy, all ratings were graded CP2, which meant that they had been able to recognise thirteen out of the first fifteen plates in the Ishihara test, which involved the picking out of numbers from plates of coloured dots; all aircrew and Seaman Officers were required to be CP1, which entailed being able to identify correctly the pairs of coloured lights emitted by a Holmes Wright lantern. If accepted, ratings were drafted to RNAS St Merryn for Basic Flying Training. Here they received battle dress blouse, trousers and beret and signed for flying clothing, an immersion suit and other safety equipment plus an extremely large holdall in which to transport it all. The prize of all prizes was signing for, and receiving, aircrew watches. These items, at that time, would make these ratings quite special within the Fleet Air Arm as Leading Rates.

The Basic Flying Training consisted of a series of lectures and flying experience, putting some of what we had learned in the classroom into practice in the air. We flew in Sea Princes for some 36 hours, carrying out radar approaches on ship contacts and land and conducting W/T exercises. The course also covered the application and use of safety equipment, firefighting, the operation of airborne cameras (which I neither saw nor heard of again), radar theory and the operation of radar equipment. The last still utilised the ASH system, which was essentially a US-designed AN/APS-4 pod installed beneath the wing for homing on to sea contacts such as a ship, a smaller vessel or a periscope. I found that, in practice, it was possible for a really well-tuned set to find and home upon quite small objects, provided the sea were calm, at quite long ranges; for example, a floating orange box could be detected at ranges of the order of 15–20 miles. The radar was also used for homing on to shorelines, but its returns, being 'B' scans, did not present a picture as on a map: the ahead-pointing system gave a display comprising a side-to-side sweep, with the aircraft's position at the bottom and centre of the screen. This screen presentation did give a peculiar representation of coastlines, but, practice making perfect, we soon became adept at finding individual headlands around that part of Cornwall, particularly the approach to St Merryn via Trevose Head.

As much basic knowledge as possible was squeezed into a few weeks' course. However, as with some other course content during service life, there were topics which, practically speaking, were of no subsequent value. Looking back, I would like to have been taught the basics of navigation and use of the mechanical Dalton computer, or its successor the 'Soup Plate'. The proudest occasion for us during that period was being awarded our aircrew Wings—something which, though not flying other than during the six years I spent in the Fleet Air Arm, I wore with pride throughout my service, even latterly for another six years as a Lieutenant. The Second Sea Lord, upon noticing them on one occasion, told me, 'If you won them, you should wear them!'

From St Merryn we were then drafted to RNAS Eglinton, the Naval Air Anti-Submarine School by the banks of Loch Foyle in Northern Ireland. Here, flying in Firefly Mk 6s and Sea Princes, we learned how to operate and use the signals received from sonobuoys to track submarines. Sonobuoys are listening devices dropped into the sea, each consisting of a cylindrical canister containing a parachute (deployed to lessen the impact when striking the sea surface), a hydrophone (an underwater microphone suspended below the buoy on a length of connecting cable) and a battery power supply, plus equipment which changes the sounds into a signal and a radio transmitter and aerial to send that VHF signal back to the aircraft. A sonobuoy's hydrophone in the water will pick up cavitation, that is, the noise of the bubbles produced from a submarine's propellers (actually, it is the noise of the bubbles collapsing that gives the sound), or, rarely, sounds from the interior of the submarine if it is close enough, and noise from other ships or objects in the vicinity, together with all sorts of squeaks and hisses, including those made by sea creatures.

Sonobuoys, laid singly or in a specific pattern, simply listen. They are not detectable by the submarine whose course and speed are being plotted. Signals from each sonobuoy we laid were then transmitted by VHF, picked up by the Gannet's receiving equipment and converted back to sound. It was the Flying Tel's rôle to determine and place on the plot the relative strength of sound from each sonobuoy, switching to the sound from each buoy in turn. This information was passed to the observer and, using this, he in turn plotted the submarine's position, course and speed, forming a determination of both the submarine's actual position and where the vessel was heading. It would then be possible to drop either homing torpedoes or a depth-charge pattern. In exercise conditions, at the end of the practice the aircraft could drop a smoke float at the expected position of the submarine and in turn the submarine would send up a smoke candle. With luck, they would coincide.

Flying from RNAS Eglinton, A/S aircraft carried out training exercises (Londonderry Joint Training exercises); examples were Stage II trainer, LJX7 and LJX9. Alernatively, there might be a Combined Anti-Submarine Exercise, CASEX, involving an actual submarine. During initial combined exercises, we were able to see, visually and on the radar screen, the radar return of a submarine's periscope, of the snorkel and of the submarine itself if it was on the surface. These exercises were co-ordinated by the joint RN and RAF centre just outside Londonderry, from where, if called for, simulated submarine cavitation signals could be transmitted without the need for the presence of an actual submarine. In normal exercise conditions sonobuoys were expected to be recovered to be used again, and so fishermen were encouraged to return the equipment if found. However, in deep-sea conditions or in remote operations, each buoy had a soluble plug which would dissolve after a certain length of time, sending the buoy to the bottom and thereby denying any enemy, potential or otherwise, the recovery of the apparatus.

The sea state, that is, its choppiness or roughness, affected the buoy's transmissions because the aerial would move violently and consequently the signals could be degraded. At times the sea state could be very poor, making reception from a buoy's transmitter quite difficult. Sea state also affected the radar returns, of course—quite dramatically if it were very bad. Nearing 'on top', over the target, for example, the radar returns were frequently swallowed up by the returns from the sea. Range had always to be estimated during the last few moments of travel, no matter what, but the figures could be increased dramatically depending on

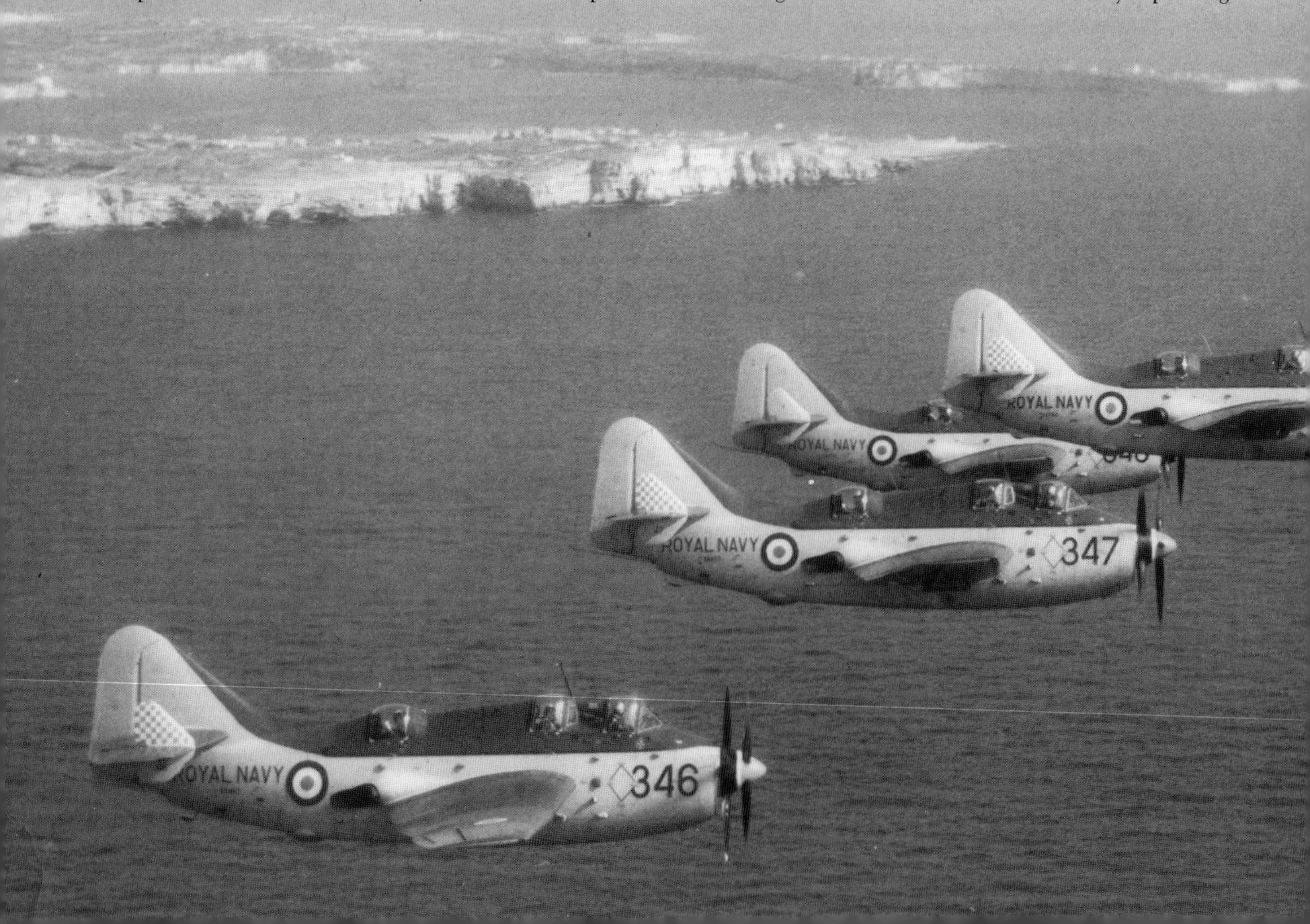

the sea state. Of course, at that stage, and indeed before, the target should have been sighted by the pilot and possibly by the observer.

From RNAS Eglinton we each went our various ways, the majority to squadrons operating A/S aircraft. I had been on two squadrons, 824 and 820 operating Avenger anti-submarine aircraft, when 820 re-equipped with Gannet A.S. Mk 1s in March 1955. Out first tasks were acceptance checks, simulated instrument flying, YG beacon approaches and flapless landings for the pilot to get used to our new aircraft. During the succeeding six months we did manage to carry out some submarine-tracking exercises, though not very many. Later, we concentrated upon single-engine and stop-engaged landings, together with A/S bombing at Minearny Range (where, incidentally, I was later to find out that the Wren Range Assessors and their colleagues, in good Irish tradition, produced a very good brew of poteen!).

The Gannet to my mind was neither an exciting nor an endearing aircraft in which to fly, and it did not bear comparison with its predecessor the Avenger, nor even with the old Dragonfly helicopter, which, for me, did have both those qualities. The aircraft was rather large and substantial, quite high off the tarmac, with a couple of footholds to climb up into the cockpit and step on to the dinghy pack before sitting down. The fuselage had a large centre-section interior which seemed to be devoid of anything except for the port and starboard exhaust tubes. Of course, there was equipment inside, but there also seemed to be lots of unused space. Beneath our cockpit, to the rear, was the retractable radome of the ARI.5838 radar—quite an exceptional set. There was also a whip aerial to pick up the signals emitted from the sonobuoys, which was moved from the near vertical to the horizontal position for landing. The rear cockpit was reasonably roomy with a good view through quite a large canopy. Facing aft and looking at that substantial tail, we Flying Tels had been told that if there was ever any necessity to bail out, we would probably hit the fin. I learnt much later that two of the crew of three in a Gannet that suffered a complete double engine failure had their arms broken when hit by the tailplane upon bailing out. As far as I remember, we only had one incident concerning that tailfin—a bird strike, about a quarter the way up. It created quite a dent in the metal skin. Our parachute was in a more normal position, at our back, compared to the Avenger's clip-on chest type.

In front of us was the sonobuoy receiver and the controls for the radar, which now had a 360-degree scan on a circular screen showing our position at its centre. This gave a Plan Position Indicator (PPI) on the screen with a map-like presentation. It was excellent for homing on to coastlines, and the returns from sea contacts ahead or astern were equally good. For whatever reason, I do not remember being given any instruction concerning the operation of this radar, nor its display. Possibly the Sea Princes, on which new trainees were being taught, had already been modified to take the new equipment and it was not thought productive to give retraining to us. Though we did carry out radar exercises, I seem to remember that they appeared to be for the benefit of the observer, not ours, carried in the back as the search radar operator. The observer had control of the lowering and raising of the radome from his cockpit.

I do remember that about this time

A seven-ship flight of 825 Squadron Gannets. COURTESY BRIAN GRINDLEY several of the Flying Tels were handed over to researchers, who sat each of us in turn in a darkened mock-up of a cockpit to look for, and report on, contacts on a radar screen that appeared at irregular intervals. Our watches were removed from us, if I remember correctly, so that we did not know how long we spent there, but it did seem to be well over an hour and possibly approaching two. The main project was punctuated by other tasks we had to perform. As is usual with the Service, we were never told of the results!

Down on the right-hand side of the cockpit (actually, the aircraft's port side, as I was rearward-facing), and running from forward to aft, were the control rods for the tailplane. It was rumoured that one of the Flying Tels had manœuvred the rods when the pilot had some difficulty in doing so whilst flying! Unfortunately, there was no direct contact between observer and the L/Tel (Air) in the rear cockpit, other than via the intercom. Thus if the observer had a message to be passed using HF radio, he had to write it down and then pass it verbally to the person in the rear cockpit via the intercom. That message, on receipt, had also to be written down again before it could be transmitted—and this was something that we had not encountered in our flying to that date. Why not? Well, for one thing, the Avenger had a tunnel connecting both cockpits; secondly, a cleft stick with a message attached to it could be used—a trifle old fashioned, but effective! The normal intercom and oxygen connections were down on the left. The Morse key was on our right-hand side. I have often wondered how left-handed 'Morse-keyers' adapted. Lower down was the chromium-plated 'pee tube'.

At this stage I must declare a bias towards American aircraft and communications equipment, particularly the latter. My first ship, HMS *Warrior*—she of the Rubber Deck and Dented Vampire—had in 1949 banks of US Navy TBM and TBL combined MF and HF transmitters in the ship's Transmitter Rooms (the former nomenclature not to be confused with the TBM Avenger aircraft!). Subsequently, several of my ships carried American HF and VHF equipment, and the former was in use right up until 1965, and possibly even slightly later, in the form of a transmitter known as 89M/P/Q. In Avenger ASW aircraft, the transmitter, AN/ART-13, was very well designed and built and had, amongst other things, ten tuneable pre-select frequencies, a good frequency coverage and an impressive 100-Watt power output. There was even a handbook to keep in a small pocket of our overalls. In retrospect I can imagine a design team discussing the basic requirements for the Gannet. 'Do they require an HF transmitter and receiver?' Those with experience of flying in the war years might have

Below: The cockpit for the A/S Gannet's 'Flying Tel' was located well aft along the fuselage—a little too near the tailfin to inspire one hundred per cent confidence in the event of a bail out being required! It was also, as Brian Grindley explains, situated very close to the Double Mamba's exhaust pipes, which on more than one occasion were the source of a fiery envelopment. This aircraft, an A.S.1, was serving with the Empire Test Pilots' School when photographed in 1955, probably at that year's SBAC at Farnborough.

COURTESY PHILIP JARRETT

replied, 'Oh yes—the aircraft can be flying low down and be quite a long way from the carrier and out of VHF touch.' 'So, what was that set that the RAF used to use? They had them in their Chipmunks. And oh yes—and didn't we have them in the Sea Princes? The TR.5206! Give them that!' So we were given a presumably newly manufactured HF transmitter and receiver in a brand new aircraft—by no means truly modern equipment.

In any case, the Service did not use any HF transmitter to anything near its full capabilities. For example, there were HF frequencies allocated to the Fleet Air Arm which were the equivalent of the then 'Bravo' frequency and certainly 'Delta' and also 'Charlie', but except for the last they were never used, the problem being the manning of the frequency on air station or carrier. Many RN air stations and carriers were fitted with FH4 (or its shipborne equivalent) HF direction-finding equipment for the purpose of triangulating and/or for finding the direction of an aircraft's or a submarine's HF transmitter, but this equipment was, to my knowledge, never used, not even in exercise.

In May 1955 I flew with our then CO, Lieutenant-Commander A. H. Smith, with Lieutenant Holliday as observer, on a search for side-number 401 (WN427), which had ditched in the sea off the north coast of Northern Ireland. That day we lost two of our aircrew, our Senior Observer, Lieutenant W. F. Molland, and our friend L/Tel (Air) 'Dizzy' Forbes. The aircraft had lost height and flown into the sea whilst attempting to 'windmill up' the second engine. All three crew members had escaped from the aircraft but only the pilot, a strong and well-built young man, got out with a dinghy. Apparently they each took it in turn to use the one dinghy, but the Senior O and 'Dizzy' became exhausted and succumbed to the cold of the sea, even though wearing immersion suits. After the subsequent investigation we were told to ensure that we clipped our lifejacket to our dinghy. Whether this had been done in the incident or whether the crew had released their dinghies to facilitate exit from the cockpits we did not know. We were also told that, in such a situation, all three crew members should occupy the one dinghy. It might be low in the water and even partially submerged as a result, but it would keep the men together and not bring about exhaustion caused by constantly getting in and out. Some of us were able to accompany 'Dizzy's coffin to Londonderry station, but as we could not all attend his funeral our Petty Officer Telegraphist (Air), Ian Curtis, went with it all the way to Dizzy's home and represented us at the service.

A similar incident occurred whilst another Gannet pilot was attempting to restart the second engine. We understood at the time that the pilot had forgotten his spectacles, borrowed some from another Squadron member but had mistakenly flown into the sea during the re-light. All three crew members got out of the aircraft, the L/Tel (Air) saying later that his intercom was switched to the radio circuit whilst operating the HF radio and that the first indication that something was amiss came when there were bumps as the aircraft hit the water and started to sink. Releasing his canopy, he had surfaced, to the surprise of the pilot and observer, who had thought that they had lost him. They had spent a while singing songs before rescuers came to their aid. I think that I might have been asking why no one had thought to tell me that we were about to ditch! Accidents of this nature always brought forth additional reminders in Admiralty Fleet Orders (AFOs), such as not to wear a tie when flying because, if the aircraft was ditching, it might strangle its wearer. We were advised also not to wear nylon socks, which could melt into the legs in the event of a fire.

During false starts, which flooded the exhaust with unburnt AVTUR, the eventual firing of the engine caused the paraffin in the exhaust to catch alight and our cockpit would be surrounded with flames. I should mention that the two exhausts, one on either side of the fuselage of the aircraft, were quite long and were internal, starting below the pilot's cockpit and running under the observer 's cockpit until they emerged just abaft my position. As the port engine was always the first to be started, any flames enveloping my cockpit were fiercest on my right-hand side—the side on which to enter and leave the cockpit . On the first occsion that this happened it was quite unexpected and somewhat worrying as I did not know how long the flames would last or if there was anything else that might catch alight. However, there was no call from the pilot to jump out—neither the pilot's nor the observer's cockpits were engulfed in flames, and the occupants probably did not even know that there was a conflagration. Someone had told us, when we first got the Gannets, that the engines were so well designed that they could run on practically anything, even powdered coal dust, as well as ship's diesel or normal AVTUR. After that first wet start we strongly doubted the coal dust!

In quiet times it was decided that we should all become qualified to sign the Gannet's A.700 for Daily and Before Flight Inspections, so after a series of lectures and practicals for all radio equipment, except the IFF, plus all electrical items, we took the examinations on the A.S. Mk I equipment—a requirement that proved useful whenever we were visiting non-RN stations or airfields abroad. We did communicate with our parent carrier by Morse, but not always. If we did, we waited until the Gannet's engines were running, then, having power, switched on the transmitter and receiver together with any other equipment, tuned to the required frequency and then set watch on the HF circuit to contact the ship's Bridge Wireless Office (BWO). The circuit would normally be operated, and controlled, by one of our Squadron's Flying Tels, not one of the ship's staff. We would ask permission for take-off by 'Q' operating signal, from Allied Communication Publication 131 (ACP131) though this had nothing to do with the aircraft actually being given clearance as the transmission was only between operator and operator.

Upon being given clearance we would then switch and return to the normal intercom position and get ready for take-off, either free or by catapult. For free take-offs we could often be spotted in the precarious position at the stern of the carrier, overhanging the round-down. Our cockpit was not actually over water, but very close to being so, the pilot often telling us that he was at 'flight idle' to maintain his position on the deck owing to the jet efflux and propeller slipstream coming from the aircraft ahead of us. My thoughts, particularly during night flying, in those conditions were with the aircraft handlers, hanging on for dear life and about to remove the chocks from the aircraft's wheels.

We always carried, in the pockets of our flying overalls, such items as maps, pencils, signal pads scrounged from the ship's BWO, a small screwdriver, possibly some aircrew rations (a small round tin of sweets) and, later on, if we were lucky enough to have obtained one, a Dalton computer—a mechanical navigation aid. The screwdriver occasionally was a necessity: it came in very handy for tightening grubscrews. For example, on take-off from a carrier we would always be on the normal intercom, but just prior to take-off we would be in touch with the carrier's BWO by Morse and the intercom switch would be in the 'radio' position. On one occasion, just prior to take-off, as I moved the intercom switch back to the normal position, the knob fell off, down into the bottom of my cockpit by my left foot; the grubscrew had become loose. After we had cleared the flight deck and I had closed my cockpit hood, the pilot asked if I was okay in the back but I could not reply to him. I then heard the pilot ask the observer if we should turn back as he could not make contact with me. The observer also tried to talk to me on the intercom. Whilst all this was going on, I had undone my harness and parachute, manœuvred myself into a position where I could just about reach down to where the knob had fallen, managed to retrieve it, replaced it in position and tightened the grubscrew with my screwdriver. I think that they were both quite relieved that I was still with them and had not passed out in the back!

On 17 September 1955, after carrying out a carrier-controlled approach, 820 Squadron's WN426, side number 404, suffered a crash on deck after landing. It was my only experience of such an occurrence, and it was quite an auspicious event as it was our very first landing on HMS *Bulwark* and we bore the 'C' of *Centaur* upon the tailfin. Landing on, we were taxying forward towards Fly One, and, upon turning right towards the carrier's deck-edge and just about to turn forward again, the Gannet's Maxarret port brake failed and we continued moving towards the deck-edge. The nosewheel went over the edge down towards the sponson below and the underside of the fuselage took the weight of the aircraft, luckily stopping any further movement. The pilot was facing seawards, with the aircraft's tail up in the air. Consequently, my cockpit was quite high above the deck. Clambering out, foremost in my mind were the Air Engineer Officer's words telling us that we Tels were always treading on a fragile, projecting exhaust from which his technicians had to knock out the dents. So, with that thought absolutely uppermost in my mind, I made sure that I did not step on that exhaust prior to jumping down. The AEO caught me in his arms. Several days later I went down into the hangar. Our aircraft had been stowed at the very rear and was looking a bit sorry for herself. I wondered what was going to happen to her, and was told that she would be cannibalised, use her for spares, until she was moved off to RNAY for full repairs. Years later I found that she had indeed been made airworthy again and had eventually been sold for scrap at Abbotsinch in 1961.

Most officer aircrew did not appear to appreciate the knowledge of communications held by an L/Tel (Air); some, indeed, did not even know that we were able to read Morse, let alone that we could read it at up to 18–22wpm and write or type it down at those speeds. One day in August 1955, as I was sitting in the cabin of a small tender off Maggilligan Point, Northern Ireland, after taking part in a Wet Dinghy Drill, over the loudspeaker came the unmistakable but muted notes of the boat's transmitter, sending the message of the time of our return to harbour. Remarking that we would be disembarking at 1155 (or whatever time it was that had been transmitted), I was asked by one of the observers how I knew. Enquiring heads turned in my direction. When told that that was what had just been transmitted, the remark was, 'Oh, can you read Morse?' Whether he and the others thought that this was just my personal expertise or that my colleagues were similarly trained I do not know. Presumably it was not appreciated that, on board ship, we were the ones to transmit and receive messages and to take radio bearings.

The L/Tel (Air) in the back was, comparatively speaking, an expert who knew the contents and rules for transmission and reception of Distress, Urgency (Pan) and Safety (*Securité*) messages, and also the 'Q' operating signals previously mentioned, from ACP131: the 'C' in ACP was for Communications, from where QFE, QNH, QGH and so on, well known to both pilots and observers, were taken. The Flying Tels knew quite a lot of these codes or operating signals by heart, and they readily acquired those dealing with flying. Cyphers as well as codes were known: we had to

Courier Tales *Lieutenant John Bewick*

The Courier Gannet was a very useful tool on board the carrier because it was the one aircraft that could disappear for the day and make available some extra space on the flight deck. The routine was therefore developed to launch the Courier Gannet at first light, and land it on again on the last recovery of daylight. To make things even easier for the flight deck engineers, on 15 April 1964 it was decided to attempt a free take-off—a new experience for everyone involved. The aircraft was spotted just about overhanging the round-down, and at full power the it used all the flight deck before it was airborne. It was not appreciated by the pilot how this looked from Flyco, who were not quite sure whether the aircraft, as viewed from above, was about to go up or down. After a number of these take-offs, the pilot was asked if he could get airborne a little bit sooner, so on the next occasion the aircraft rotated as soon as it was felt it would fly, took off in the vicinity of the after lift and climbed steeply so that it was at least level with the Flyco windows as it passed by. This take-off gave a fright not only to the pilot but also to the Powers That Be, and he

Above: The accident that befell WN426 on board HMS *Bulwark* in September 1955.

be well versed in the reception and transmission of such messages, and in messages dealing with enemy reporting—Initial, Amplifying, Negative, Raid and so on—together with the very important 'Submiss' and 'Subsunk' signals.

My next Gannet squadron was 825 at RNAS Culdrose in A.S. Mk 4s, in January 1958, moving out to RNAS Hal Far half way through the month. I often flew with our USN exchange pilot, Lieutenant-Commander Hattersley, a former dive-bomber pilot . Out there we flew in formation over HM aircraft carriers *Eagle* and *Ark Royal*, and on other occasions searched for them or shadowed them and then carried out low-level 'strikes' against them.

We must have had some Gannet fuel problems during February 1955 as I see that we carried out several fuel flow check flights and that, following these, during a CASEX 41 that we were conducting with a submarine, we had to return to base because of a fuel overflow. At this time in the Mediterranean we carried out more anti-submarine exercises than we had done for many a month. Having Filfla nearby, upon which we could carry out live dive-bombing and RP firing, was quite a change. However, all good things have to come to an end, and it was decided in April 1958 that the Squadron should return home, leaving me behind to transfer to 728 Squadron, flying in Sturgeons and Meteor T.T.20 target-towing aircraft. Here was something quite new to learn!

---

was asked to return to the old method of take-off. According to records, the Courier Gannet was the last fixed-wing aircraft in the Royal Navy regularly to undertake free take-offs from a flat-top carrier.

The Courier, a Gannet A.S. Mk 4 stripped of operational equipment, was a one-off type on board, so had its own servicing crew of one CPO plus four, together with the pilot, and all six personnel were involved at times in servicing the aircraft. One of the problems discovered involved the clamp ring that held the exhaust pipe to the engine. This ring managed somehow or other to spin, causing a great deal of wear on the flanges of both the exhaust cone and the exhaust pipe. The problem was eventually rectified by wire-locking the clamp so that it could not move.

The only engine failure I experienced with the Courier was during a flight to collect the mail from RAF Akrotiri in Cyprus. The cause was a failure of the main bearing and the consequential contamination of the engine oil. There were a number of factors which made this event memorable. The Officer Commanding RAF Akrotiri took the view that the aircraft had to fly to and from his airfield and that, therefore, the engine should be changed there. However, HMS *Victorious* had a date with the Suez Canal, which meant that she had to leave the area by 1.00 a.m. the following morning in order to join the convoy through the waterway. It

COURTESY JOHN BEWICK

COURTESY RICHARD L. WARD

COURTESY PHILIP JARRETT

Above: Gannet C.O.D Mk 4 XA430 carrying out wire-pulling trials on board HMS *Victorious* in 1966.

Left, upper: XA430 was one of the very first Gannets to be assigned to the COD rôle. Originally unmarked following conversion, it was allocated to HMS *Ark Royal* as part of the so-called 'COD Flight'. In due course all COD Gannets were transferred to the custody of 849 Squadron.

Left, lower: XA466 served in the courier rôle before being wholly converted to C.O.D. Mk 4 standard. Equipped with an updated communications suite but for the time being retaining its radar 'dustbin' and Extra Dark Sea Grey/Sky colour scheme, it is seen here in 1963, when, amongst its other duties, it served as a courier aircraft for HMS *Hermes*.

Opposite, top: COD Gannet XA454, assigned to Flag Officer Aircraft Carriers, makes a free take-off from HMS *Victorious* in early 1964.

COURTESY JOHN BEWICK

would not be possible to change the engine ashore in the time available.

The Staff Air Engineering Officer was flown ashore and disappeared in the direction of Nicosia, 'to see what he could do', and a few hours later sent a message that he had found a lighter which could transport the Gannet to the ship. It was found that the Army had a crane about three miles from the airfield suitable to lift the Gannet and swing it out over the water to the waiting lighter, if it could get there in time. The next problem was to remove the Gannet from the clutches of the RAF and tow it out of the main gate and down the road—a task accomplished with inches to spare. We always wondered what would have happened had there been an accident on the crane—operated by the Army, on a Naval aircraft, under the ground control of the RAF towing team, on to a lighter owned by a civilian by the name of Ali. Who would have been responsible for raising the A.25? The Gannet was lifted on to the flight deck with half an hour to spare!

COURTESY 'PAF' GRANT

Left: Naval humour, never in short supply, frequently expressed itself in the form of cartoons, and Lieutenant 'Paf' Grant was a particularly wry observer of life in the Fleet Air Arm. This contemporary drawing reflects on the incident at RAF Akrotiri described on these pages by John Bewick.

MAINTENANCE

Commander Simon Askins

MAINTENANCE for the Gannet A.S.1s and 4s was carried out according to a timed schedule of weekly, monthly and quarter-year checks, modified by periods of non-flying when the time was suspended. These 'Mainchecks', numbered 1 to 5, were progressively more detailed examinations of the structure and components, and of course a number of defects were delayed for rectification until a convenient servicing period came around.

By the time the A.E.W.3 came along in the early 1960s, the RN had changed its servicing philosophy as it realised it was grossly 'over-maintaining' its aircraft fleet and thereby consuming far more manpower than was necessary. The system was replaced by a new 'Flexible Servicing' system which broke down the blocks of inspections into 'bite-size' pieces which could be done in a few hours after flying had been completed for the day. Naturally, some tasks were more complex and occasionally necessitated an aircraft being in the hangar for a few days. Major items such as an engine change, scheduled or not, would be used as an opportunity to carry out other major tasks at the same time. An engine change would take only some ten hours from start to finish. Generally, this system did improve availability and reduce the number of man-hours spent on servicing.

At infrequent intervals aircraft were withdrawn and returned to the manufacturer for reconditioning. By the time the A.E.W. Mk 3s required this procedure, Westlands had taken over major support for the Gannet. The company then needed a suitable place to overhaul the airframes and test-fly them, and it decided on the simple expedient of using a large hangar at RNAS Yeovilton already rented from the Royal Navy for use on earlier jet aircraft contracts. This was but ten miles from the company's main factory at Yeovil, which had only a grass airfield, unsuited to Gannet flying. Yeovilton at least had all the facilities needed, and was thenceforward referred to by the company as Westlands, Ilchester. Aircraft were usually flown in but if unflyable (for example, after an accident) would travel on a low-loader provided by the Navy's own movement service.

The Gannet was somewhat large for a low-loader, however, and considerable dismantling was required, together with a special cradle to hold the fuselage on the truck. It had to be craned on, and set at an angle of about 40 degrees of bank in order to reduce the width. The tailfin, too, had to be removed. The fuselage was designed in three sections—front, ahead of the wings; centre, including the stub mainplanes; and rear, including the tailplane unit. The degree of dismantling depended on the nature of any damage and the route that had to be taken (for example, whether overhead bridges had to be negotiated). Westlands—later to become Westland Helicopters (WHL)—also had a helicopter facility at Weston-super-Mare on the Somerset coast, where Gannets could be flown in for minor work or servicing.

While undergoing reconditioning, the aircraft would be completely disassembled, each section and item of equipment being sent for appropriate

VIA AUTHOR

servicing. This meant that, when aircraft were in the process of reassembly, it was not uncommon for parts from several different Gannets to be incorporated in the target fuselage. The resultant aircraft when re-issued would be, in effect, 'as new'. This also applied when heavily damaged aircraft were 'reduced to spares and produce': the repairable parts were fully reconditioned and then re-used. Repaired or refurbished aircraft would then be returned to the Aircraft Holding Unit at RNAS Culdrose.

The worldwide deployment of the fleet carriers meant that reserve aircraft of all types had to be kept 'in theatre' to provide quick replacements for any losses. The Royal Navy had a holding unit at Singapore (at RAF Changi), and spare, serviceable aircraft were sent out on merchant vessels or Royal Fleet Auxiliaries. These aircraft had to be fully protected against weather and humidity and so were cocooned in plastic coverings. This preparatory work was often carried out at RNAY Fleetlands, Gosport, which, although not set up to service or fly Gannets, could put them into preservation for shipping. Once in the Far East, the aircraft were unpacked and then kept serviceable and fully modified, to be available at short notice for issue to any carrier that needed a replacement.

Back home, the move from RNAS Culdrose to Brawdy meant that from being the only fixed-wing squadron on a station operating helicopters, 849 was now one among many fixed-wing squadrons. At Brawdy was the main Naval Aircraft Support Unit

Below: The final phase of the maintenance schedule was to test-fly the aircraft—to its limits—to ensure that it would perform as it should. Here Gannet A.E.W. Mk 3 XL500 is put through its paces during a test flight.

(NASU), which quickly added the Gannet family to its repertoire of Sea Vixens, Scimitars, Sea Devons, Meteors and Vampires that were accepted for Level 4 maintenance (major inspections) from the Fleet and air stations to be worked on, test-flown and then held for re-issue.

There was a dedicated team of Air Engineering Officers and ratings working in the NASU under Commander (E), Bill Myers, with specialist AEOs for each aircraft type. Lieutenant Dennis Sharpey was the Gannet 'guru'. The efforts of the resident team were supplemented if required by working parties from the manufacturers or the RN mobile repair team (MARTSU) to tackle crash repairs and major defects such as structural cracks.

The final stage from the overhaul lines was, of course, the test flight, and there were two or three resident Maintenance Test Pilots on the station who were qualified to fly all these types of aircraft. They were also available to assist squadrons by carrying out the annual test flights on all aircraft, and with trouble-shooting. During my time there, I learned my Gannet 'folklore' from the extrovert engineer pilot RQF (Bob) Evans—known to all by his self-proclaimed Welsh moniker 'Evans the Test'—who was also an enthusiast for the Swordfish and his own vintage Humber car.

The test pilots were all ex-front-line pilots, in addition to being qualified AEOs, and were experienced to handle any in-flight flight emergencies. This was just as well: over the years we came across just about every engine, hydraulic, electrical and avionic emergency possible. I personally experienced the ultimate emergency

COURTESY GEOFF WAKEHAM

Below: The result of the author's unorthodox landing at Withybush on 13 March 1967, as described in the text. Burnt paint may be seen along the engine cowling.

Above: A forlorn XA363, an A.S.1 once used by the Maintenance Test Pilots' School at Abbotsinch (the crest for which can just be discerned at the fin-top), in the fire pit at Culdrose in June 1973.

when during a test flight, a double engine fire developed (shown to have arisen from a combining gearbox failure following an alternator seizure). The remedy was to stop both engines and use the fire extinguishers—which cured the fire but gave a false and temporary impression of quiet calm. Fortunately, there was a disused airfield (Withybush, in South Wales) within what I judged to be gliding distance from my 5,000-foot height, and I declared my intention of landing there. My observer, Lieutenant Bryn Moore, elected to abandon the rear cockpit and try his parachute. Encouraged by a colleague who offered beer as a reward for making it, I did manage to land, using the emergency hydraulic reservoirs to put down the undercarriage and flaps late on the approach. The exercise would have finished up better had there not been a sheep fence fixed across the runway which removed the aircraft's nose leg! To demonstrate that we were not unduly worried by this event, Bryn and I flew the aircraft on its first flight after repair.

AUTHOR'S COLLECTION

GANNET TRAINING

Commander Simon Askins

SOME pilots and observers progressed naturally to the Gannet from the anti-submarine versions of the Firefly. These personnel were well accustomed to carrying out ASW patrols, albeit with very early-standard equipment. The Firefly could fly for a maximum of about four hours and the Gannet could manage about the same (more with a bomb-bay tank or, in the A.E.W.3, drop tanks under the wings) while carrying a greater payload of avionics and weaponry and an additional crew member. The last Fireflies were replaced by Gannets in 1956.

New Gannet pilots were selected from the training 'pipeline' once they had been awarded their 'wings' while their counterparts were sent for fast-jet or helicopter training. This meant that they had probably been trained on Vampires at either RAF Linton-on-Ouse or RAF Valley (which posed some problems, as Bryan Sarginson relates opposite). A few aircrew would have been flying the Sea Venom. Early variants of this aircraft were not equipped with ejection seats, and when the Mk 21 came along, which did have them, it was found that some aircrew, both pilots and observers, were too tall to fly the aircraft: there was insufficient room for their knees to miss obstructions as the seat exited. The answer was to re-train on the Gannet, which could accommodate the tallest crew as either pilot or observer.

The first pilots for the Gannet Mk 1 were sent to Armstrong Siddeley for a week of instruction on the engines, their operation, and the starting sequence. Following this they went to Fairey at Hayes for air-frame ground school and a good look at the aircraft being built and test-flown. They were allowed to start an aircraft at White Waltham, although of course not to fly one as the aircraft were not at that point the property of the Royal Navy. It was a couple of years before Fairey produced the first of the T.2 trainers (converted A.S.1s), and later on there was a batch of new-build T.5s, which were essentially A.S.4s with a second set of flying controls but no radar. Happily, the operation of the engines was virtually identical for all Gannets, irrespective of

Below: Techniques and tactics relating to anti-submarine warfare were taught to Gannet crews on 719 Squadron, the Naval Air Anti-Submarine School, based at RNAS Eglinton. Here eight Gannet A.S.1s of the Squadron fly over the coastline of Northern Ireland. It may be noticed that not all the aircraft are fully crewed.

COURTESY PATRICK ROGERS

Expensive and Damaging Things *Commander Bryan Sarginson*

I was at RNAS Eglinton in Northern Ireland on 737 Squadron and just starting my Gannet training. One Saturday I was sent off in a T.2 trainer for my third solo to do local familiarisation and a few circuits. Returning to the airfield, I can now recollect that I had used the 'flat' Vampire approach technique for my first attempt at a 'touch and go' landing. The Gannet, however, preferred a steeper approach path, and indeed this was advisable at Eglinton as a railway line and embankment crossed the runway threshold a fair bit above runway level. The consequence of this was that I 'clipped' the railway, which did several expensive and damaging things to my Gannet, most of which were not clear until after my eventual landing!

The nose oleo had hit first and been pushed right back to the fuselage. The front prop had bent back so that its blades were hitting the rear prop. The main undercarriage legs sheared off, with one totally gone the other left dangling by its hydraulic pipery. I had been briefed that, if I was not happy with the approach, I should go round again. So I did, rather hoping—and in ignorance of the severity of the damage—that nobody would have noticed my error. A further problem, however, was that the impact had put all the electrics off-line, killing many of the instruments and the radio; the 'crash switch' had tripped. Thus I climbed away with the engines and propellers protesting madly and making a noise the like of which had never been heard before.

As I circled, sorting myself out, another Gannet with an instructor in it came alongside and made a number of gestures, none of which meant anything to me (there are no hand signals meaning 'Your entire undercarriage has been destroyed'). So I continued. The landing had to be on the belly in the absence of any undercarriage—and, to my surprise, the entire air station seemed to have come out to watch!

After considerable debriefing (and an eyesight test), I was sent back aloft again to continue my course. I later served on other Gannet squadrons ashore at Eglinton and Culdrose and in 815 Squadron embarked in HMS *Ark Royal.*

mark. Eventually a procedure trainer was installed at Eglinton, which, if lacking the sophistication of a full simulator, did allow engine handling to be practised, including all emergency routines. This was carried forward to the A.E.W.3 variant in due course, the trainer moving from Culdrose to Brawdy in the mid-1960s.

The pilots meanwhile were appointed to the first squadrons to form, 826 at RNAS Lee-on-Solent and 824 at RNAS Culdrose in, respectively, January and February 1955, followed in March by 737 (Training Squadron) and 820 at RNAS Eglinton. This meant that these men were instructed verbally by the trials squadron pilots and learned the emergency procedures from the Pilot's Notes.

The Observer Training School had been based at RNAS St Merryn (HMS *Curlew*), where 796 Squadron were based with Fireflies and Sea Princes until the end of 1953. It then moved to RNAS Culdrose. The Telegraphist Air Gunners (TAGs) were being trained on the communications and weapons systems on 744 Naval Air Squadron at RAF St Mawgan. Training was not without incident: the crew of WN371, for example, on a transit flight from 796 NAS at Culdrose in December 1956, suffered total engine failure at 15,000 feet. The engines could not be restarted and aircraft ditched in the sea, although, happy to relate, the pilot and his crew were rescued.

In 1960 the Observer Training School moved out to Malta from Culdrose to take advantage of the better weather. The students stayed for eighteen weeks at RNAS Hal Far and then returned to Culdrose for a further five months with the Headquarters element of 849 Squadron, which was responsible for Operational Conversion Training on type for the new pilots and observers. The observers did time in the AEW Intercept Trainer and had 120 hours' flying in the A.E.W.3 with a qualified observer-training officer. On completion of this, they were awarded their 'Wings'. 849 was at Culdrose until December 1964, then moved to Brawdy and in November 1970 moved again, this time to RAF Lossiemouth. It was disbanded in 1978 on the decommissioning of HMS *Ark Royal.*

A Gentleman's Aircraft

Commander Tony Shaw MBE

I did not fly the Gannet in first-line operations: my experience of this aircraft is confined to weapon-handling trials in 1954 during my time in 'C' Squadron at Boscombe Down and later, in 1960–61, when I was CO of 700 Squadron, the Service Trials Unit.

I regarded the Gannet as a fine piece of engineering. The management of the twin engines was of absorbing interest in the operation of its many and varied rôles. Sitting comfortably in this well-planned cockpit, with the distinctive and friendly purr of the turboprops, and with an excellent all-round view, made for joyful flying at its best With such a superb view ahead, and with good stability on the approach, this was the simplest deck-landing aircraft I had known.

In 700 Squadron we employed several types of aircraft for the varied tasks in which we were engaged. One of these was to provide pilots and aircraft for the deck trials of our carriers (of which there were many) when they were newly commissioned, or as they emerged from refit. We would spend up to a week on board whilst the arrester gear and catapult launching systems were proved and the deck and hangar handling teams were worked-up. As Squadron CO I would always exercise my right to choose the aircraft type to fly in each element of the trials programme. When the Gannet was required, that was always my choice!

Of all the joys of the Gannet, the greatest for me was to be accompanied by a Fleet Air Arm observer. After nineteen years flying single-seaters, or on my own, having someone there to do all the hard work was an experience to be relished. The Gannet was a gentleman's aircraft, with gentlemanly characteristics—and I loved it!

EXPERIENTA DOCET

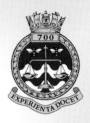

700 NAVAL AIR SQUADRON

Located at RNAS Ford and, from 19/09/58, at RNAS Yeovilton

Commissions
18/08/55–03/07/61 (Gannet A.S.1s throughout, at least one T. 2 briefly in 1955 and A.S.4s 00/02/57–00/02/60)

Commanding Officer(s)
Lt-Cdr R. W. Turral, Lt-Cdr D. G. Halliday (16/01/56), Lt-Cdr P. M. Lamb DSC AFC (23/01/57), Lt-Cdr T. G. Innes AFC (27/080/57), Lt-Cdr R. A. Shilcock (29/09/58), Lt-Cdr A. I. R. Shaw MBE (12/09/60)

Senior Pilot(s)/Senior Observer(s)
Lt-Cdr S. Farquhar (SP in 1955)

COURTESY BRIAN LOWE

COURTESY BILL HARRISON

Left: 700 Squadron was the initial trials and intensive flying trials squadron, tasked with evaluating the Gannet. Many hours were flown on a limited number of airframes and engines to ensure that there were no obvious problems before the type was introduced to front-line service. The Squadron worked in parallel with 703X Flight (q.v.). XA411, a Gannet A.S.1 of 700 Squadron, is seen here at Ford (whose station code is displayed on the tailfin) in late 1956, at which time it was carrying the call-sign '522'. The finlets are tipped in Extra Dark Sea Grey—an unusual touch—and the colour separation line around the tailplane differs from the standard later adopted.
Above: With the move to RNAS Yeovilton in 1958, the tail code letter was changed; the finlet *décor* was retained. This is XG832, an A.S. Mk 4.
Below: 700G Flight was the intensive flying trials squadron for the Gannet AEW Mk.3. It had on strength several early-production aircraft, including XL456 seen here at Brawdy. The unit, its primary work completed, was redesignated the Headquarters element of 849 Squadron as the Gannet took over the airborne early warning task on the front line from the Skyraider.

700G FLIGHT

Located at RNAS Culdrose
(became HQ Flight 849 NAS on disbandment)

Commissions
17/08/59–01/02/60 (Gannet A.E.W.3s throughout)

Commanding Officer
Lt-Cdr W. Hawley

Senior Pilots/Senior Observers
Lt-Cdr W. H. Barnard (SP), Lt-Cdr S. McGrail (SP), Lt-Cdr A. W. Roberts (SObs), Lt-Cdr R. Coventry (SObs)

COURTESY PHILIP JARRETT

Intensive Flying Trials

Admiral Sir Desmond Cassidi GCB

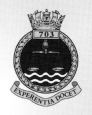

703X FLIGHT

Located at RNAS Ford

Commission
15/03/54–21/12/54 (Gannet A.S.1s throughout)

Commanding Officer
Lt-Cdr F. E. Cowtan

Senior Pilot(s)/Senior Observer(s)
Lt-Cdr A. D. Cassidi (SP)

I was told in 1953 that I was being appointed as the Senior Pilot of 703X Flight, which was being formed to conduct the Intensive Flying Trials of the Fairey Gannet prior to the aircraft's entry into squadron service. The Flight was stationed at RNAS Ford under CO Lieutenant-Commander Frank E. Cowtan. The aim was to achieve 100 hours of flying on each of four aircraft, exercising, as far as possible, the various rôles of which the aircraft was capable. After preliminary acquaintance courses at Fairey Aviation on airframes and handling, and with Armstrong Siddeley for the engine, we received the aircraft—WN347, '348, '349 and '350, in March 1954. The Fairey test pilots Group Captain Gordon Slade and Lieutenant-Commander Peter Twiss helped with the initial check-outs.

The initial goal of 100 hours' flying was achieved with few problems. At this stage each aircraft had an engine change, and the trials were to be repeated for another 100 hours on each. It was during this phase that some problems began to be encountered. The angled deck concept had just been adopted, and so in the course of conducting ADDLs attention was being given to engine response on 'round again' action in the event that an aircraft missed a wire. It was found that if the throttles were operated too quickly, it was possible to stall the engine(s)—which would be disastrous on board a carrier. This problem was reported but Boscombe Down, who had done some experimental work on the aircraft, tended to discount the incidents, which, following the successful first 100 hours phase, seemed to indicate some sort of engine installation difficulty. However, after visits from experts at Fairey and Boscombe Down to Ford, it became apparent that some rectification was necessary, and a delay mechanism in the throttle operation was introduced.

During this second phase one aircraft was selected for hot-weather trials in Khartoum, where a small RAF unit

COURTESY RICHARD L. WARD

COURTESY BRIAN LOWE

provided support. The aircraft, fitted with a long-range tank, was flown out without incident. Instrumentation was fitted, and there was a special Flight Observer for the trials—the well-known Miss Lettice Curtiss, who had been an ATA pilot during World War II. Once the trials had been completed, arrangements were made to conduct some 'touch and go' landings on HMS *Albion*, which was fitted with an 'interim' 5-degree angled deck and a mirror sight. An RV was made in the Med, and this programme, too, was completed successfully.

Meanwhile the work at Ford continued and the time came for a series of deck trials in the Channel. Two aircraft landed on HMS *Albion* and were turned round and prepared for catapulting. The first Gannet was launched successfully, but the second, WN348, suffered an engine stall as it went off the catapult and, with wheels down and flaps down, just failed to maintain height and ditched ahead of the carrier. Unfortunately, the Flight Observer, Mr J. D. Byrne from RAE, was lost. After much investigation—and the grounding of the Flight's aircraft—it was determined that the problem was associated with the fuel layout of the Double Mamba, specifically where the fuel pipe to the front of the engine extended along the top from the back: the amount of 'g' exerted by the catapult forced the fuel back along the pipe, causing fuel starvation and engine stall. The shortcoming was rectified by the insertion of a 'dashpot' of fuel to the front of the engine, providing enough fuel for the Mamba to recover from the 'g' effect.

Soon after this the trials were completed and the Flight dispersed to join squadrons being equipped with new aircraft as they became available. Fairey had also built a trainer version of the aircraft, and I collected the first of these, WN365, and flew it to RNAS Eglinton to assist with checking out pilots for 820 and 824 Squadrons re-forming there.

Broadly speaking, the Intensive Flying Trials proved their worth; indeed, the practice of establishing an IFTU for new aircraft was continued. A lot was learned by the maintainers as well as by the aircrew, and all the activities were carefully monitored to be included in instructions for squadrons. So far as I know, no catapult faults had been noted in any of the experimental establishments. No particular armament trials or drops were carried out by 703X Flight, but exercise sonobuoy patterns were dropped using smoke floats. I do not recall flying on any 'live' submarine exercises.

All the pilots found the Gannet a joy to fly, with good sight lines for the deck and a roomy cockpit (although the observer's and TAG's stations were more cramped). But for being overtaken by the 'dunking choppers', the Gannet would have been a thoroughly successful anti-submarine aircraft.

Left: Formed at Ford with Gannet A.S.1s—three of which are seen here—703X Flight was the first unit to fly have regular squadron pilots flying the aircraft. It conducted intensive flying trials and deck-handling evaluation, investigating also hot-weather trials (for which it was detached to Sudan) and cold-weather operations (in Canada). The Flight was disbanded once the trials had been completed.
Above and right: WN348—which appears also nearest the camera in the photograph at left—was one of the early Gannets issued to 700X Flight, but the aircraft served only for a few months as it was written off in a launch accident during trials on board HMS *Albion* in August 1954, as described by Admiral Cassidi on these pages. As far as can be ascertained, 703X's Gannets carried no unit identity markings to decorate the standard postwar Fleet Air Arm finish of Extra Dark Sea Grey and Sky Type 'S'.

COURTESY BRIAN LOWE

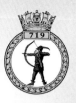

COURTESY PATRICK ROGERS

719 NAVAL AIR SQUADRON

Located at RNAS Eglinton

Commission
14/06/50–17/03/59 (Gannet A.S.1s and T.2s from 00/11/55)

Commanding Officers
Lt-Cdr J. D. Nunn, Lt-Cdr E. R. A. Johnson (11/01/56), Lt-Cdr A. W. Sabey DSM (06/08/57), Lt-Cdr D. L. G. James (13/12/57), Lt-Cdr A. A. Reid (21/01/59)

Senior Pilot(s)/Senior Observer(s)
Lt-Cdr P. R. Dallosso (SP 13/12/57–00/02/58)

Left: A flight of 719 Squadron A/S Gannets up from Eglinton. This unit, otherwise known as the Naval Air Anti-Submarine School (or, later, the Naval Anti-Submarine Operational Flying School), was the first of the Gannet training squadrons and took delivery of the aircraft from 1955, supplanting its Fireflies.
Below: Gannet trainers were immediately distinguishable not only by the periscope above the instructor's cockpit but also, generally speaking, by their colour scheme—'silver' overall, relieved by training bands in yellow or, later, larger areas of 'dayglo' orange-red. Individual squadron markings were sometimes worn, as on this 719 NAS aircraft, XA510.
Opposite, top: Another image from the 719 Squadron sortie depicted above. The unit's *décor* was characterised by red and black spinners and red and black chequers on the rear of the upper finlets; the lower surfaces of the finlets bore an abbreviated form of the aircraft side numbers or call-signs.

COURTESY BILL HARRISON

COURTESY PATRICK ROGERS

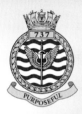

737 NAVAL AIR SQUADRON

Located at RNAS Eglinton

Commission
30/03/49–22/11/57 (Gannet A.S.1s and T.2s from 00/03/55)

Commanding Officers
Lt-Cdr D. W. Pennick,
Lt-Cdr R. D. R. Hawkesworth DSC (03/05/56)

Senior Pilot(s)/Senior Observer(s)
Not known

COURTESY BILL HARRISON

Above: 737 Squadron, also based in RNAS Eglinton was, like 719, a component of the Naval Air Anti-Submarine School and of the 53rd Training Air Group (TAG). When it disbanded in 1957 its aircraft were transferred to 719 NAS. This is A.S.1 WN405 in inclement weather at Blackbushe in 1959, with an engine cowling that has clearly been 'borrowed' from a T.2 trainer.
Below: XA508, a Gannet T.2 trainer on the strength of 737 Squadron. A colour photograph of this same aircraft appears on page 97.

COURTESY PHILIP JARRETT

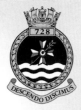

728 NAVAL AIR SQUADRON

Located at RNAS Hal Far

Commission
08/05/43–31/05/67 (one Gannet T.2 00/07/57–00/11/57)

Commanding Officer
Lt-Cdr R. C. B. Trelawney

Senior Pilot(s)/Senior Observer(s)
Not known

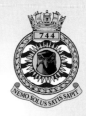

744 NAVAL AIR SQUADRON

Located at RAF St Mawgan

Commission
01/03/54–31/10/56 (Gannet A.S.1s 00/05/55–00/10/56)

Commanding Officers
Lt-Cdr F. G. J. Arnold, Lt-Cdr R. Fulton (04/01/56)

Senior Pilot(s)/Senior Observer(s)
Not known

728 NAS was a training squadron for observers and aircrewmen. It moved to Hal Far in 1957 with 750 Squadron (Sea Princes) as the Observers' Training School and also provided aircraft for the Fleet Requirements Unit there, using Meteors and Sturgeons and, for a few months in 1957, a Gannet T.2. 744 NAS was part of Naval Air–Sea Warfare Development Unit based at RAF St Mawgan (with the Shackletons there), flying A.S.1s; in addition, it trained Naval Telegraphist Air Gunners (TAGs) for a period. 796 NAS, based at Culdrose, was part of the Observer Training School, flying A.S.1s and T.2s.
Right: Officers of 796 Squadron (CO Lieutenant-Commander Don Moore-Searson, seated centre) at Culdrose immediately prior to the unit's disbandment in 1958.
Below: WN377, an early A.S.1 used by 796 NAS.

COURTESY DON MOORE-SEARSON

COURTESY BILL HARRISON

COURTESY HELEN CLARKE

Above: A hitherto unpublished photograph of a trio of 847 Squadron Gannet A.S.1s on a sortie from their base at RAF Nicosia in Cyprus in 1957. This unique Gannet establishment was formed at RNAS Eglinton specifically for service in the eastern Mediterranean, its task to watch for foreign shipping that might be 'gun-running' to the EOKA terrorists during the unrest that was being experienced on the island for much of the 1950s. The A.S.1s were in due course replaced by A.S.4s, and the Squadron generally had three aircraft serviceable at any time.

Below: XA508, a Gannet T. Mk 2 of 737 Squadron in—for the most part!—the standard trainer finish of the 1950s.

BILL HARRISON

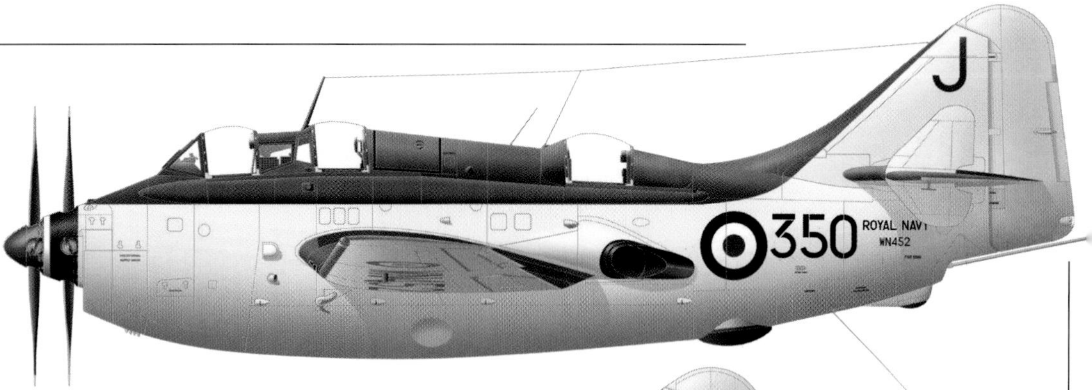

Fairey Gannet A. S. Mk 1 WN452, 826 Naval Air Squadron, HMS *Eagle*, June 1955

Fairey Gannet A. S. Mk 1 WN426, 820 Naval Air Squadron, HMS *Bulwark* (*sic*), September 1955

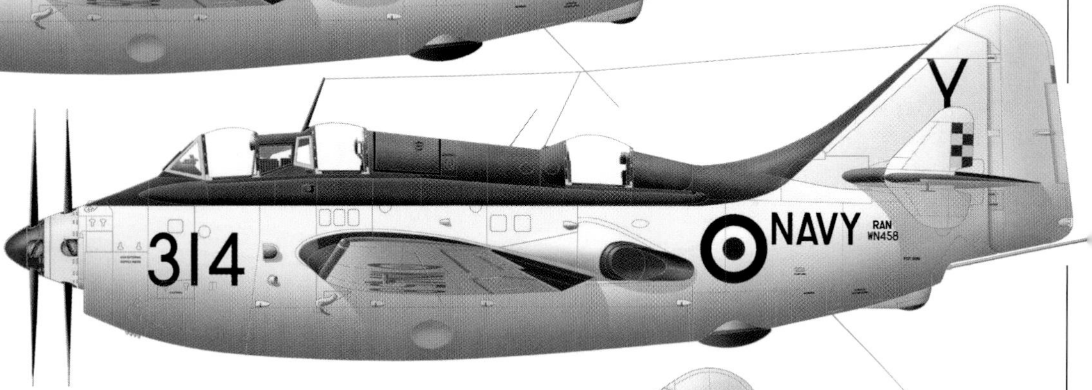

Fairey Gannet A. S. Mk 1 WN458, 817 Naval Air Squadron, RNAS Culdrose, January 1956

Fairey Gannet A. S. Mk 1 XA347, 719 Naval Air Squadron, RNAS Eglinton, February 1956

Fairey Gannet A. S. Mk 1 WN371, 812 Naval Air Squadron, HMS *Eagle*, April 1956

Fairey Gannet T. Mk 2 XA514, 724 Naval Air Squadron, NAS Nowra, October 1956

Fairey Gannet A. S. Mk 1 XA400, 1840 Naval Air Squadron (Channel Air Division), RNAS Ford, October 1956

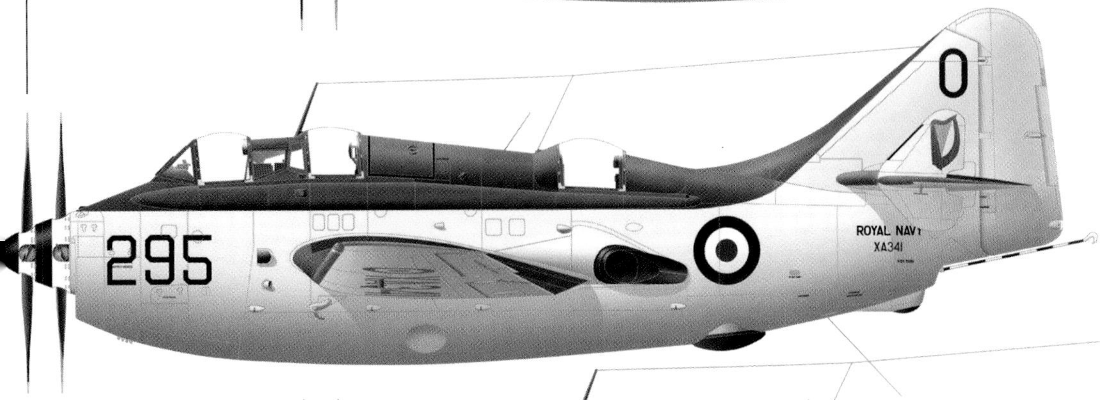

Fairey Gannet A. S. Mk 1 XA341, 815 Naval Air Squadron, HMS *Ark Royal*, January 1957

Fairey Gannet A. S. Mk 4 XA418, 824 Naval Air Squadron, HMS *Albion*, February 1957

Fairey Gannet T. Mk 2 XA524, 820 Naval Air Squadron, RNAS Eglinton, February 1957

Fairey Gannet A. S. Mk 1 XA411, 700 Naval Air Squadron, RNAS Ford, March 1957

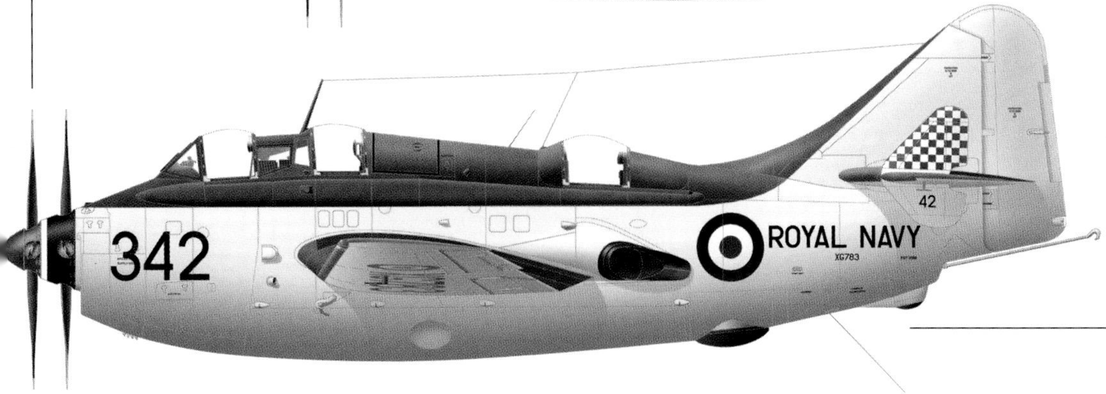

Fairey Gannet A. S. Mk 4 XG783, 825 Naval Air Squadron, RNAS Culdrose, May 1957

RCO8

FLOWN BY THE AUTHOR

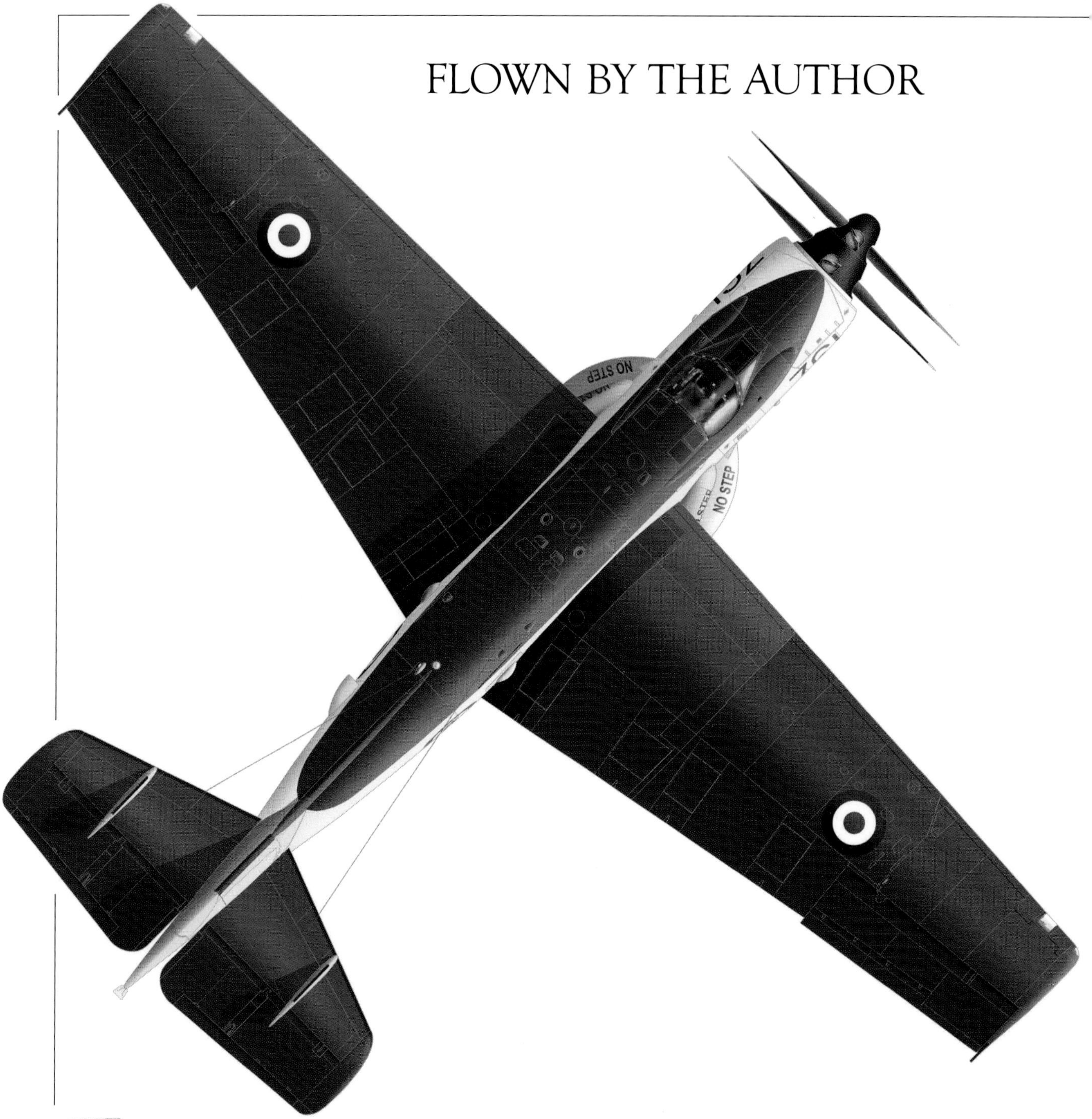

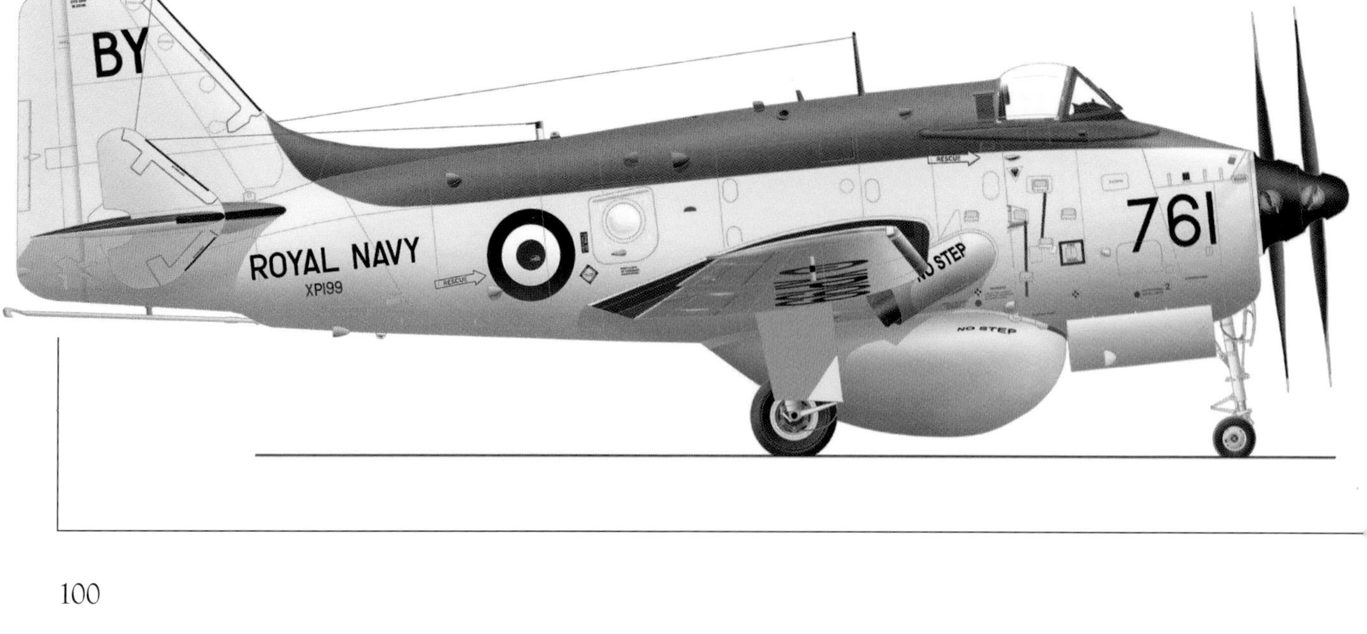

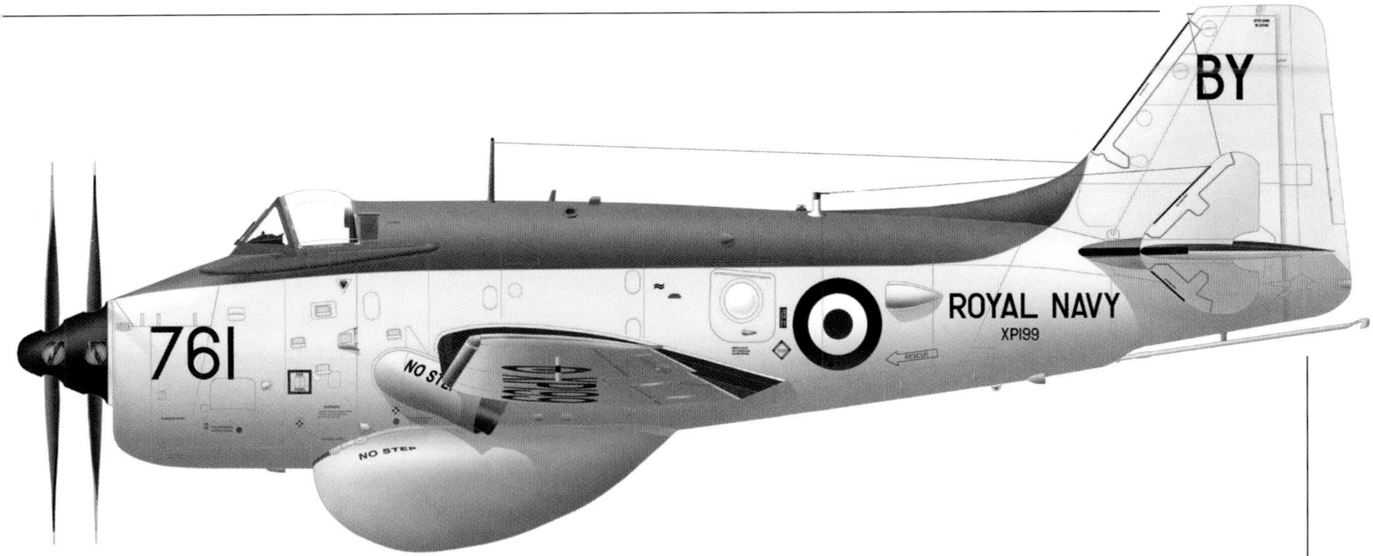

FAIREY GANNET A.E.W. Mk 3
XP199, HQ Flight 849 Naval Air Squadron, RNAS Brawdy, May 1966

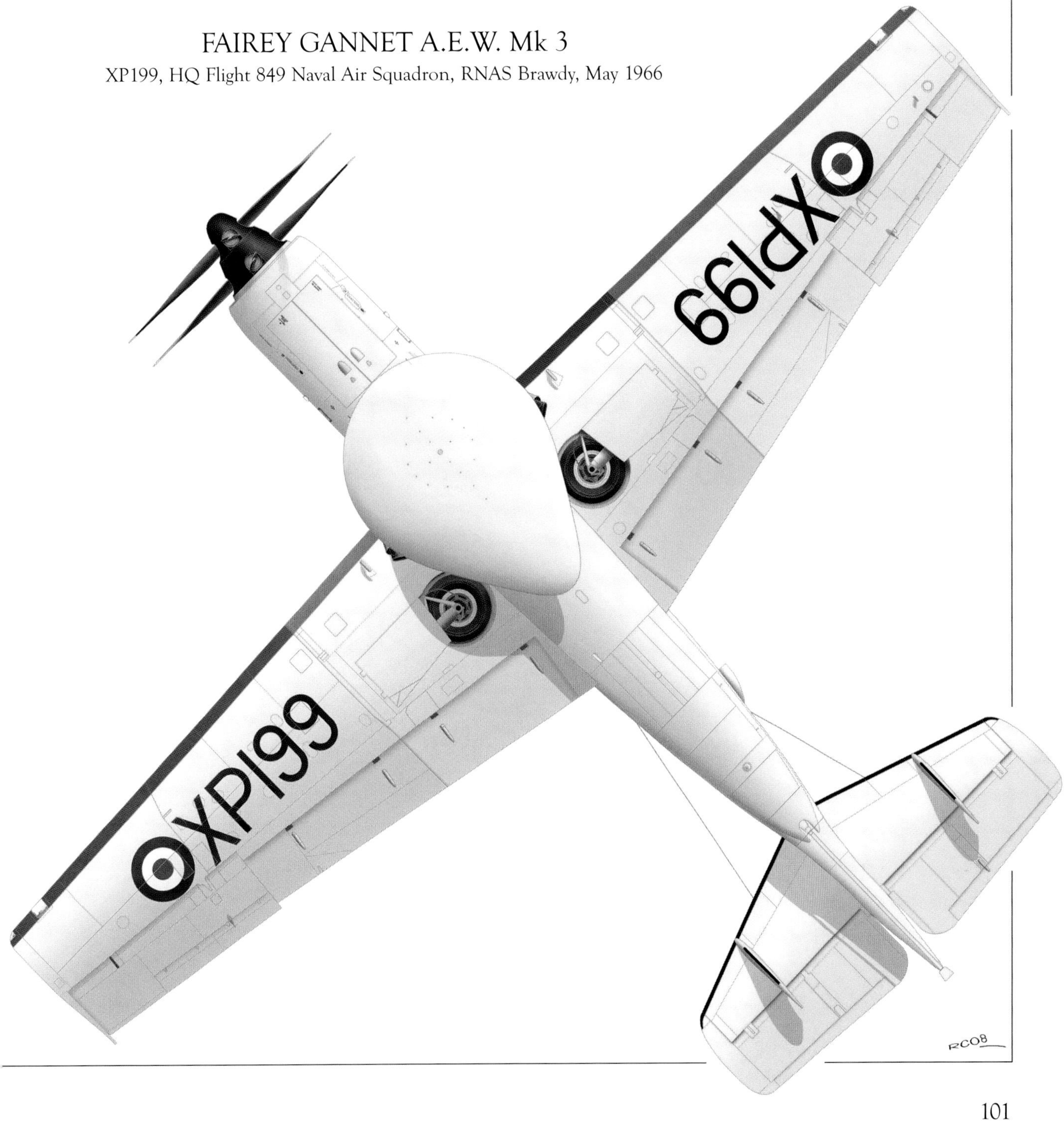

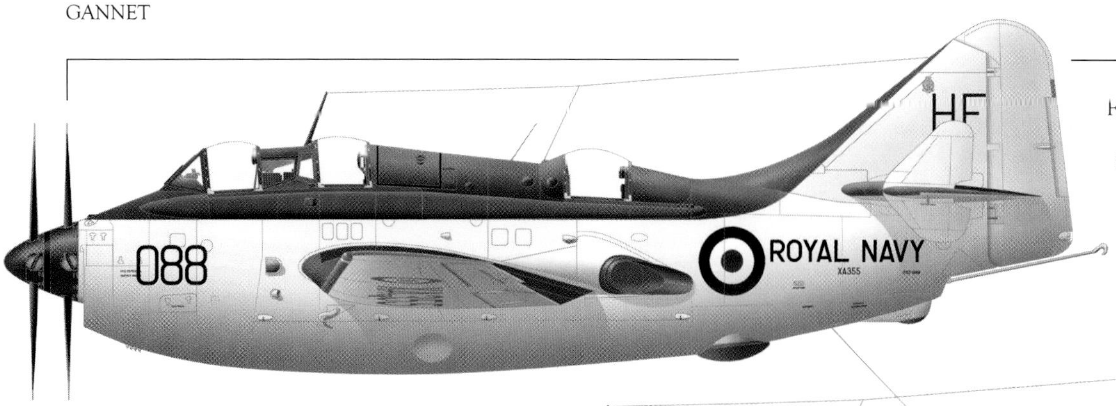

Fairey Gannet A. S. Mk 1 XA355, 847 Naval Air Squadron, RAF Nicosia, November 1957

Fairey Gannet A. S. Mk 1 WN359, 796 Naval Air Squadron, RNAS Culdrose, January 1958

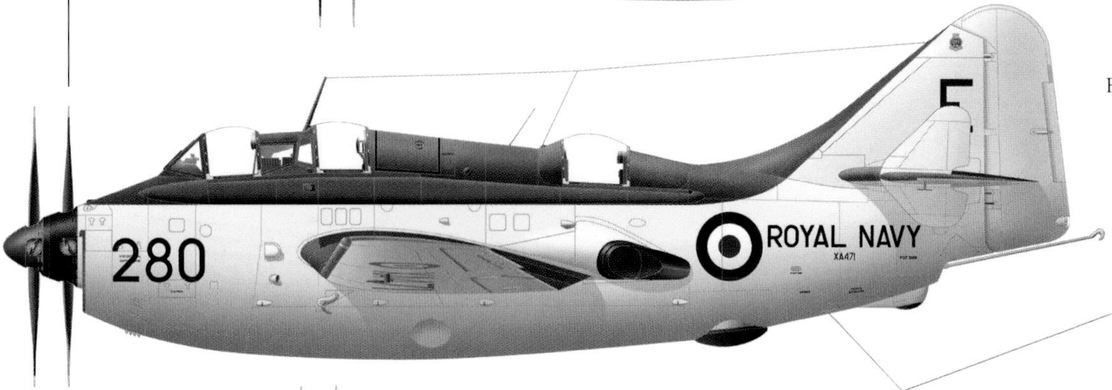

Fairey Gannet A. S. Mk 4 XA471, 814 Naval Air Squadron, HMS *Eagle*, June 1958

Fairey Gannet A. E. W. Mk 3 XL471, 'C' Flight 849 Naval Air Squadron, HMS *Hermes*, October 1960

Fairey Gannet A. S. Mk 4 XG789, 816 Naval Air Squadron, HMAS *Melbourne*, August 1961

Fairey Gannet C. O. D. Mk 4 XA454, Ship's Flight (Flag Officer Aircraft Carriers), HMS *Victorious*, January 1965

Fairey Gannet E. C. M. Mk 6 XA459, 831 Naval Air Squadron, RAF Watton, September 1965

Fairey Gannet C. O. D. Mk 4 XA470, Ship's Flight, HMS *Hermes*, January 1967

Fairey Gannet A. E. W. Mk 3 XL503, 'A' Flight 849 Naval Air Squadron, HMS *Victorious*, January 1967

Fairey Gannet A. E. W. Mk 3 XL481, 'D' Flight 849 Naval Air Squadron, HMS *Eagle*, October 1970

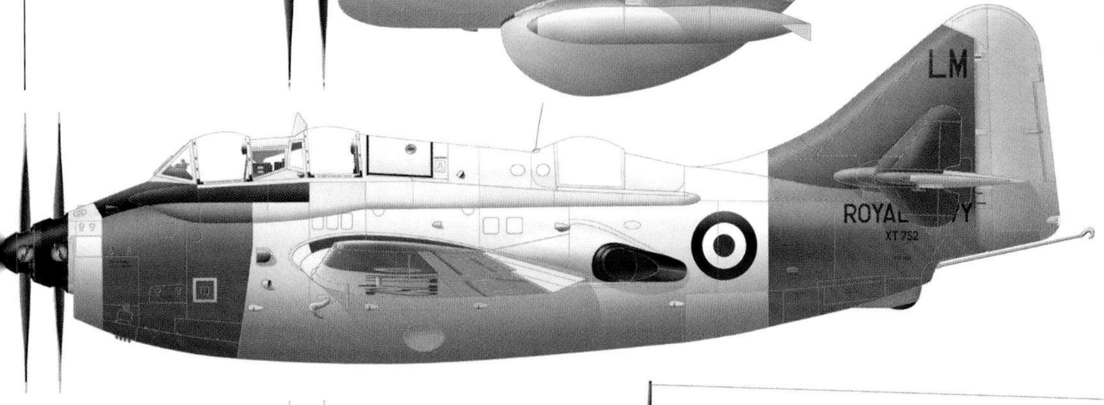

Fairey Gannet T. Mk 2 XT752, HQ Flight 849 Naval Air Squadron (Gannet Support Unit), RNAS Lossiemouth, May 1972

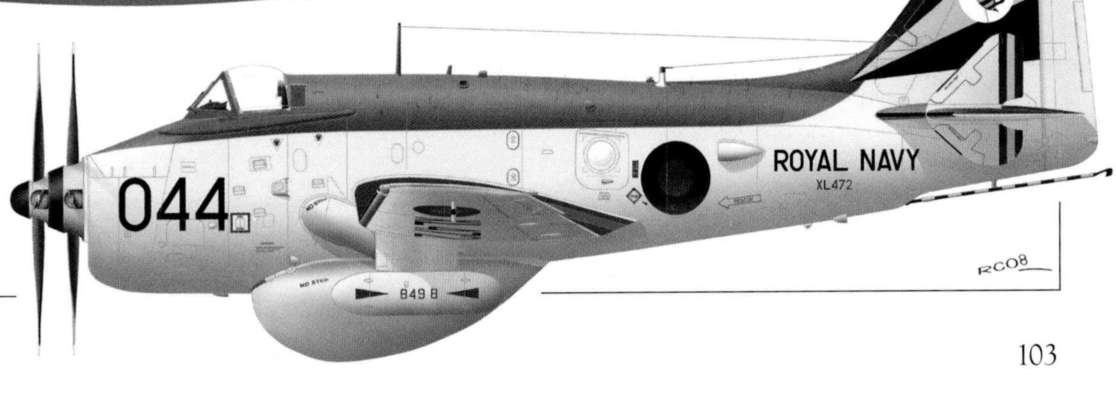

Fairey Gannet A. E. W. Mk 3 XL472, 'B' Flight 849 Naval Air Squadron, HMS *Ark Royal*, February 1976

LOU LOMHEIM

Left: A.E.W.3 XP226 (through the 'porthole') from the observer's station on the starboard side of an accompanying Gannet Mk 3. The aircraft is demonstrating single-engine flying and wears the markings of 'A' Flight 849 Squadron in 1962. The tail code, 'C' for *Centaur*, partially visible, is carried unusually low on the fin.

RICHARD L. WARD

Left: 'B' Flight 849 Squadron's Gannet Mk 3 XL502 performs a high-drag slow fly-by for the benefit of air show spectators.

Below: A rather faded Gannet A.E.W.3—XL472 late of 'B' Flight 849 Squadron on board *Ark Royal*—on display at the Gatwick Aviation Museum in 2007.

AUTHOR

Right: Eye-catching, synchonised engine starts were not the sole prerogative of the Fleet Air Arm's Sea Hawk fighters: not to be outdone, 796 Squadron's Gannets could put up a spectacular display too, as seen in these photographs taken during the 1958 Air Day at Culdrose. At that time 796 was the largest unit in the FAA with a strength of 24 aircraft, but later that year it, like dozens of other squadrons, would receive the order to disband as a direct result of the British Government's perception that the age of the guided missile had arrived and that manned aircraft other than transports were therefore no longer required.
Below right: Lieutenant-Commander Don Moore-Searson, the last CO of the last Gannet A/S training squadron, gazes nostalgically at one of his aircraft. The device on the finlet is the 'Cornish pirate' emblem adopted by the Squadron.
Bottom: Derelict ex-796 Squadron Gannets photographed at RNAS Abbotsinch a year after they were withdrawn from service.

COURTESY DON MOORE-SEARSON

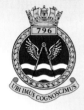

COURTESY DON MOORE-SEARSON

796 NAVAL AIR SQUADRON

UBI IMUS COGNOSCIMUS

Located at RNAS Culdrose

Commission
13/11/47–01/10/58 (Gannet A.S.1s and T.2s from 00/02/57)

Commanding Officers
Lt-Cdr W. L. Hughes, Lt-Cdr A. H. Smith (06/01/58), Lt-Cdr L. D. Moore-Searson (10/01/58)

Senior Pilot(s)/Senior Observer(s)
Lt-Cdr P. J. Spelling (SP in 1958)

COURTESY DON MOORE-SEARSON

COURTESY BILL HARRISON

Gannets at Nowra *Lieutenant-Commander Peter Dallosso*

I joined 724 Squadron (CO Tony Robinson RAN) as Senior Pilot in 1955. The Squadron, based at Nowra, New South Wales, trained newly qualified pilots prior to entering front-line units. The Sea Fury/Firefly years had ended and the Vampire/Venom/Gannet years just started. I was already Vampire-qualified, and I quickly undertook the Gannet conversion course at Nowra.

The syllabus was the usual spread of type conversion, IF, navigation, weapons, night and dummy-deck work. I found the Gannet a pleasant aircraft to fly, with an excellent view and well-harmonised controls. It introduced me to my first front-line aircraft autopilot—and 45-degree banked turns were great fun! Flying from the instructor's position took a little practice, as the view forward was through a periscope and, generally, one had to get used to the idea of flying a twin-engined aircraft on one engine—intentionally!

I was involved in an accident with Gannet T.2 XA514 on 13 November 1956. The endorsement in my Log Book tells most of the story:

'NAS Nowra's 130746Z Gannet T.2 XA514. While accompanying test pilot on maintenance test flight after ECU change, port PCU failure caused overspeed on port engine which shut down but would not feather. Aircraft returned to Nowra and undercarriage was lowered. Propeller went to fine pitch and 'disced'. Airspeed lost and aircraft carried out emergency landing alongside non-duty runway with undercarriage not locked down. Test pilot's error in not engaging Flight Fine Pitch Stops.

'[Signed] J. A. Gledhill, Cdr RAN'

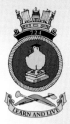

724 NAVAL AIR SQUADRON

Located at NAS Nowra

Commission

01/06/55–30/06/84 (Gannet A.S.1s 00/06/55–00/01/58 and 00/05/61–00/07/64, T.2s 00/06/55–00/01/58 and 00/05/61–00/11/66)

Commanding Officers

Lt-Cdr L. A. Robinson RAN, Lt-Cdr P. R. Dallosso (18/02/57), Lt K. M. Barnett RAN (01/07/57) Lt-Cdr A. G. Cordell RAN (06/08/57), Lt-Cdr C. E. Champ RAN, (01/09/58), Lt-Cdr G. H. G. Hanchard-Goodwin (01/12/58 and 20/07/59), Lt-Cdr M. W. M. Barron (15/02/59 and 31/10/60), Lt-Cdr I. K. Josselyn RAN (09/12/59), Lt-Cdr M. E. Lee RAN (03/02/61), Lt-Cdr A. E. Payne RAN (01/06/61), Lt-Cdr J. P. van Gelder RAN (22/06/62), Lt-Cdr A. Ignatieff RAN (15/07/63), Lt-Cdr M. J. Astbury RAN (01/08/65), Lt-Cdr K. A. Douglas MBE RAN (23/08/65)

Senior Pilot(s)/Senior Observer(s)

Lt-Cdr P. R. Dallosso (SP to 17/02/57)

COURTESY PETER DALLOSSO

My part in the accident was more active than this endorsement reads. I was flying as second pilot in the instructor's position to check everything in that cockpit. The failure occurred almost immediately after take-off. The test pilot turned left downwind and lowered the undercarriage. He said nothing to me or to ATC. After a time—it seemed an age but was actually about 30 seconds—I took over control. The turbulent airflow from the two propellers at cross purposes affected tail-end control somewhat and speed was all the while decreasing, so I turned the aircraft towards the grass, got the undercarriage going up and belly-landed across the airfield. The test pilot still said nothing, and following my report he was taken off flying.

On completion of my interesting and enjoyable appointment at Nowra, I returned home and was appointed Senior Pilot to 719 Squadron (CO D. L. James) at Eglinton at the end of 1957. This squadron was busy on Gannet training, crew training and working-up crews with ships. The appointment was hectic, enjoyable and short. Early in 1958 the AFO came round announcing defence reductions and calling for volunteers to retire. I made my last flight in the RN on 26 February 1958 in Gannet A.S.1 WN450: '20° R/P; GCA; circuits; gentle flypast. 1hr 15 mins.'

A final anecdote trom 719 Squadron. On 16 January 1958 I had the pleasure of checking out Commander E. M. ('Winkle') Brown in the Gannet. After the appropriate dual, he went off solo. On his return I asked him how the flight went: 'Fine, thanks—and that was my 294th type!' was his reply.

COURTESY PETER DALLOSSO

Above: 724 Squadron officers in October 1956: (seated, left to right) Lieutenant-Commander Dallosso (SP), Lieutenant-Commander Robinson (CO) and Lieutenant Oldham; (standing) Lieutenants Lee, Anderson, Lister, Coker-Godson (AEO) and Reid. The Squadron crest—or a variation of it—appears on the Sea Venom in the background.
Left: Squadron headquarters at Nowra, with three Sea Venoms, two Vampire trainers, three Gannet A.S.1s and, in the hangar, a Gannet trainer. By late 1956 the Squadron also had a couple of Bristol Sycamore helicopters.

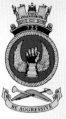

BE AGGRESSIVE

725 NAVAL AIR SQUADRON

Located at NAS Nowra

Commission
13/01/58–31/05/61 (Gannet A.S.1s and one T.2 throughout)

Commanding Officers
Lt-Cdr J. M. Wade-Brown RAN, Lt-Cdr K. M. Barnett RAN (04/08/58), Lt-Cdr P. Goldrick RAN (29/07/59), Lt-Cdr A. E. Payne RAN (27/07/60)

Senior Pilot(s)/Senior Observer(s)
Not known

FRONT-LINE SQUADRONS

Commander Simon Askins

ONCE full production of the Gannet was under way, squadrons formed in fairly quick succession and were soon deployed to their carriers. This was helped by the fact that the first crews to form were all fully experienced in the equivalent Firefly A/S aircraft, so it was just a question of their becoming familiarised with the Gannet before becoming fully operational.

Squadrons formed at the naval air stations at Ford (Sussex), Lee-on-Solent (Hampshire), Culdrose (Cornwall) and Eglinton (Northern Ireland). The last two named had resident training squadrons, which provided the new crews for the 'parented' front-line units.

The front-line squadrons had individual identities, generally reinforced by coloured markings applied to the aircraft. The favoured positions for these markings were the tail finlets and the propeller spinners. In addition, aircraft carried a ship or station identity letter on the tailfin, plus a squadron number which was its in-flight call-sign. The tailfin letter matched the flight-deck letter painted on the carriers, port side aft and either amidships or to starboard forward, on the deck. As squadrons

formed and disbanded and their aircraft were reassigned, these numbers and letters of course had to be changed accordingly. Newly delivered aircraft from either the manufacturer or an aircraft repair yard were usually devoid of any markings except their airframe (serial) number, applied either side of the rear fuselage, and under each wing, and the usual panel identity and warning notices.

The naval air stations, too, had letter identities—'CU' for Culdrose, 'GN' for Eglinton, 'FD' for Ford and 'LP' and later 'LS' for Lee-on-Solent in the case of the Gannet units—applied to the tailfins of their aircraft, while the resident (usually second-line and training) land-based squadrons had their own distinctive side numbers. Shore bases operating Gannets comprised, in addition to those above-mentioned, Bramcote ('BR'), Brawdy ('BY'), Hal Far (Malta) ('HF'), Lossiemouth ('LM'), Nowra (Australia) ('NW') and Yeovilton ('VL').

The tasks, deployments and establishments of the various Gannet front-line squadrons are covered (in numerical order) in the following pages.

Below: Gannet Mk 3 '070' of 'D' Fl;ight 849 Squadron takes off from *Eagle* for a dawn patrol.

COURTESY PHILIP JARRETT

COURTESY PHILIP JARRETT

Left: HMS *Ark Royal* undergoing trials on the English Channel in October 1955 prior to her Mediterranean cruise, with three 824 Squadron Gannets seen aft. Two dark blue Skyraiders are also present, and Sea Hawks line the flight deck to port and starboard. A Whirlwind helicopter is positioned at the bows. The ship's identity letter, 'O', is evident forward of the round-down on the port side. Right: 820 NAS provided the anti-submarine protection on board HMS *Centaur* ('C' forward and aft) in 1956, and four of the Squadron's Gannet A.S.1s are seen here aft. Below: HMS *Albion* in January 1956, with five Gannet A.S.1s of 825 Squadron and three AEW Skyraiders of 849 Squadron ranged aft and Sea Hawks and Sea Venoms amidships. The identity letter aft is here partially concealed by one of the Gannets.

COURTESY PHILIP JARRETT

US NAVY COURTESY A. D. BAKER III

810 NAVAL AIR SQUADRON

Located at RNAS Culdrose, RNAS Hal Far *et alibi* and on board HMS *Centaur*

Commission
20/04/59–12/07/60 (A.S.4s throughout)

Commanding Officer
Lt-Cdr A. McK. Sinclair

Senior Pilot(s)/Senior Observer(s)
Not known

Having disbanded as a Sea Hawk squadron engaged in the Suez operation of 1956, 810 NAS recommissioned at RNAS Culdrose as a Gannet squadron in April 1959 because the newly arrived Whirlwind helicopters were proving unreliable. The last of the anti-submarine squadrons to form, it operated Mk 4s only until July 1960.

Below: XA473 of the Squadron, showing its characteristic red front spinner.

Left, lower: Squadron personnel: (left to right), Jem Tetley, Vic Sirett, (unidentified), Neil Foster, (unidentified), Sub-Lieutenant Elcock, (unidentified), Sandy Sinclair (CO), Joe Jones, Noel Unsworth, Sub-Lieutenant Pringle, (unidentified) and Jim Flindell; (kneeling) Chris Jarman, Nick Gent and Kim Halley.

Right: HMS *Centaur* at speed in 1959, showing off her new 6-degree angled deck and steam catapults, and her air group of 801 NAS Sea Hawks, 891 NAS Sea Venoms and—partially obscured by the top hamper—810 NAS Gannets. Not visible here are the ship's 849 NAS 'D' Flight Skyraiders.

VIA AUTHOR

VIA AUTHOR

COURTESY JOHN BEWICK

COURTESY DICK OINN

812 NAVAL AIR SQUADRON

Located at RNAS Eglinton, RNAS Hal Far and RNAS Lee-on-Solent and on board HM Ships *Bulwark* and *Eagle*

Commission
07/11/55–13/12/56
(A.S.1s throughout, one T.2 until 00/03/56)

Commanding Officer
Lt-Cdr G. D. Luff DFC

Senior Pilot(s)/Senior Observer(s)
Not known

From being a night fighter squadron in Korea and disbanding in 1953, 812 Squadron re-formed on 7 November 1955 at Eglinton with Gannet A.S.1s and a T.2 for continuation flying when disembarked. The Squadron embarked in HMS *Eagle* in April 1956 as the anti-submarine force. However, with the coming of the Suez Crisis, it was replaced on board by strike fighters and disembarked to Hal Far in case a submarine threat emerged (it did not). It returned home and disbanded in December 1956.

Opposite page: Pilot, observer and TAG disembark from WN368 and deck handlers go about their work amongst A.S.1s of 812 Squadron in the deck park on board *Eagle* in 1956. A single Wyvern of 830 Squadron is parked at the bow, to starboard, and this has a Sea Hawk behind it. Most of the Gannets have RP rails underwing.

Below: 812 Squadron markings were restricted to black spinners, as here on WN400 displaying its ASV radar 'dustbin'; although not evident in this early photograph (but readily discernible in that opposite), most Gannets, throughout most of the commission, also wore the unit crest beneath the 'J-for-*Eagle*' code letter on the fin.

Bottom: An 812 Squadron Gannet Mk 1 is catapulted from HMS *Eagle* somewhere in the Mediterranean in 1956. Sea Hawks line the starboard deck edge.

COURTESY ERIC COOP

COURTESY DICK OINN

814

IN HOC SIGNO VINCES

814 NAVAL AIR SQUADRON

Located at RNAS Culdrose, RNAS Eglinton and RNAS Hal Far and on board HMS *Eagle*

Commission
14/01/57–30/09/59
(A.S.4s throughout, one T.2 until 00/02/57)

Commanding Officers
Lt-Cdr R. Fulton, Lt-Cdr J. J. Phillips (04/01/58), Lt-Cdr G. D. H. Sample DSC (12/09/58), Lt-Cdr D. C. Eve (01/05/59)

Senior Pilot(s)/Senior Observer(s)
Not known

COURTESY BRIAN LOWE

COURTESY RICHARD L. WARD

Left: 814 Naval Air Squadron is a front-line anti-submarine unit of long standing, equipped firstly with Fireflies, then with Gannets, subsequently with Wessex and Sea King helicopters and currently (2008) with Merlin helicopters. It re-equipped with Gannet A.S.4s at RNAS Culdrose in January 1957. Here XA468/'287' is coming in to land on board HMS *Eagle*, with a second aircraft in the circuit, about half a minute behind. The ship has only just completed her turn into wind.

Above: The Squadron embarked in *Eagle* in August 1957. XA426 is seen here semi-recessed in the carrier's forward lift well. Unusually, the rear propeller spinner appears to be medium blue; the normal finish was blue forward and black aft. XA432 is nearby.

Below: Gannet A.S. Mk 4 XG783 about to touch down on board HMS *Eagle*, the aircraft's arrester hook caught at the precise moment of its engagement with the wire.

COURTESY BRIAN LOWE

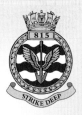

815 NAVAL AIR SQUADRON

Located at RNAS Eglinton, RNAS Culdrose and RNAS Hal Far and on board HMS *Ark Royal*

Commission
06/02/56–15/07/58 (A.S.1s until 00/12/57, then A.S.4s; one T.2 until 00/09/56)

Commanding Officers
Lt-Cdr J. P. David, Lt-Cdr J. K. Mortimer (20/07/57)

Senior Pilot(s)/Senior Observer(s)
Not known

Based in Northern Ireland since World War II, 815 NAS re-formed at Eglinton with Gannet A.S.1s in February 1956 taking most of the crews from Fireflies; sensibly, it quickly established an association with the makers of a well-known Irish stout and carried the relevant harp motif in green on the finlets of its aircraft.

Below: A.S.1 XA336 on board *Ark Royal*.

Right: XA338, also a Mk 1, demonstrates its prowess with the release of a homing torpedo.

Bottom: 815 Squadron Gannets in summer 1957 during cross-operations with the USS *Saratoga*, two of whose Skyraider attack aircraft are seen at right. The Gannets' spinner colours are black and white.

COURTESY PHILIP JARRETT

COURTESY BILL HARRISON

COURTESY BRIAN LOWE

COURTESY PHILIP JARRETT

Main image: A flight from 816 Squadron (Royal Australian Navy) during their working-up at RNAS Culdrose in summer and autumn 1955. The Squadron operated seven aircraft, their tail codes originally 'B' (as here) but changing to 'Y' the following year and finally 'M' in 1957 (all signifying HMAS *Melbourne*).
Left and below: XG787 of the Squadron operating from HMAS *Melbourne*. In Australia the Gannets were home-based at RNAS Nowra, NSW, where the training squadrons were also located.

MAIN IMAGE: COURTESY ROYAL AUSTRALIAN NAVY

ROYAL AUSTRALIAN NAVY, COURTESY BILL HARRISON

Right: The second RAN squadron, 817, formed and worked up at RNAS Culdrose in 1955 with 816. Both squadrons embarked in the then-new HMAS *Melbourne* for passage back to Australia. The Squadron's distinctive *décor* comprised a red front spinner and a yellow rear, with chequers in the same colours on the finlets. This is WN458.

COURTESY BILL HARRISON

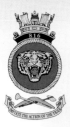

816

IMITATE THE ACTION OF THE TIGER

816 NAVAL AIR SQUADRON

Located at RNAS Culdrose and NAS Nowra, and on board HMAS *Melbourne*

Commission
15/08/55–25/08/67
(A.S.1s throughout, T.2s 00/03/59–00/10/63)

Commanding Officers
Lt-Cdr B. G. O'Connell RAN, Lt-Cdr P. Goldrick RAN (00/00/57), Lt-Cdr J. Griffin MVO RAN (05/08/57), Lt-Cdr D. C. Johns RAN (12/01/59), Lt-Cdr K. M. Barrett RAN (16/06/61), Lt-Cdr A. E. Payne RAN (22/06/62), Lt-Cdr T. A. Dadswell RAN (02/12/63), Lt-Cdr M. J. Astbury RAN (01/11/56)

Senior Pilot(s)/Senior Observer(s)
Not known

817

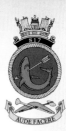

AUDE FACERE

817 NAVAL AIR SQUADRON

Located at RNAS Culdrose and NAS Nowra, and on board HMAS *Melbourne*

Commission
18/08/55–18/08/58 (A.S.1s throughout)

Commanding Officers
Lt-Cdr J. A. Gledhill DSC RAN, Lt-Cdr J. S. Hickson RAN (00/11/56), Lt-Cdr H. E. Bailey DSC RAN (07/01/57)

Senior Pilot(s)/Senior Observer(s)
Not known

820 NAVAL AIR SQUADRON

Located at RNAS Eglinton and RNAS Sembawang and on board HM Ships *Bulwark* and *Centaur*

Commission
07/03/55–15/06/56, 30/07/56–02/12/57
(A.S.1s throughout, T.2s from 30/07/56)

Commanding Officers
Lt-Cdr A. D. Cassidi, Lt-Cdr A. H. Smith (18/05/55), Lt-Cdr D. O'D. Newbery (30/07/56)

Senior Pilot(s)/Senior Observer(s)
Not known

Another anti-submarine squadron of long standing, 820 was equipped with early-production Gannets. Home-based at Eglinton, it embarked in HMS *Centaur* in early 1956 but later that spring its aircraft went in for upgrade and storage at RNAY Donibristle. The squadron re-formed again at Eglinton with later-standard A.S. Mk 1s in July 1956 and embarked in *Bulwark* in June 1957.

Below: XA396 on board *Bulwark*. 820's unit markings comprised purple and white spinners and finlets.

Right: XA534, a T.2 trainer with 820 NAS in 1956–57. It is finished in the standard trainer scheme of the day—'alumunium' overall with yellow wing and fuselage bands—but has the Squadron colours applied to the spinner.

COURTESY PHILIP JARRETT

COURTESY BRIAN LOWE

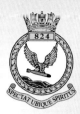

824
SPECTAT UBIQUE SPIRITUS

824 NAVAL AIR SQUADRON

Located at RNAS Eglinton, RNAS Brawdy, RNAS Hal Far, RNAS Ford and RNAS Culdrose *et alibi* and on board HM Ships *Bulwark*, *Ark Royal* and *Centaur*

Commission
18/02/52–17/04/56, 07/05/56–01/11/57 (A.S.1s 00/02/55–17/04/56, 07/04/56–00/10/56; A.S.4s 00/10/56–01/11/57; T.2s 00/04/56–00/12/56)

Commanding Officers
Lt-Cdr J. D. Honywill (11/01/55), Lt-Cdr L. D. Urry (11/05/56)

Senior Pilot(s)/Senior Observer(s)
Not known

Right: Four aircraft of the Squadron seen during the first Gannet commission, when the side numbers, in the 411–419 range, were carried aft. Below: 824 disbanded at Ford in April 1956, only to re-form at Culdrose the following month, initially with Mk 1s although these had been replaced with A.S.4s by October that year. Call-signs were changed, and repositioned on the aircraft, as shown in this view of A.S.4 XA418 making a free take-off from HMS *Albion* (code 'Z') in the first half of 1957. The pilot's and observer's canopies are closed; the TAG is, clearly, less confident about matters!
Right, lower: The Gannet was noted for its capacious bomb bay, which could carry just about anything. This included the proverbial kitchen sink—as members of 824 Squadron proved one day in 1956. CO 'Joe' Honywill is seen here with the actual projectile (believed to be inert—probably a practice kitchen sink) and surrounded by Squadron personnel who include the bearded AWI, Sean McGrail.

COURTESY PHILIP JARRETT

VIA AUTHOR

VIA AUTHOR

825 NAVAL AIR SQUADRON

Located at RNAS Culdrose, RNAS Sembawang, RNAS Ford and RNAS Hal Far and on board HMS *Albion*

Commission

04/07/55-07/08/56, 06/05/57-29/04/58 (A.S.1s until 07/08/56, A.S.4s from 08/05/57, T.2s 00/10/55-00/12/55 and 06/05/57-29/04/58)

Commanding Officers

Lt-Cdr A. H. Smith, Lt-Cdr J. R. C. Johnston (00/00/55), Lt-Cdr R. C. Ashworth (06/05/57), Lt-Cdr R. Leonard MBE DFC (23/02/58)

Senior Pilot(s)/Senior Observer(s)

Lt-Cdr R. Leonard MBE DFC (SP 00/00/57-22/02/58), Lt-Cdr V. Hawes (SObs in 1958)

825 NAS, having in its recent past been a Firefly fighter squadron and then a Firefly anti-submarine squadron, formed again in July 1955 in order to operate Gannet A.S.1s. Shore-based at Culdrose, it embarked in HMS *Albion* in January 1956 for the Far East but disbanded a few months later at RNAS Lee-on-Solent. It re-formed again the following year at Culdrose with nine Gannet A.S.4s, was based at RNAS Hal Far, Malta, for nearly a year thereafter and finally disbanded at Culdrose at the end of April 1958.

Right: The Squadron's red and white chequerboard markings can be made out on the finlets in theis photograph of a 'finger-four', but the aircraft lack tail codes. It was apparently Squadron policy to change the paintwork on the propeller spinners of its Gannets from time to time: in April 1957 (when this photograph was taken) they were red with a central white band but a few weeks later the front spinner was white and the rear red. Later, the spinners of 825's Gannets had red forward and black aft of the white central band (see next photograph and those overleaf).

Below: Officers of the Farnborough display team: (back row, left to right) Pat Symons, Pat Rogers, Peter Fish, John Taylor, Don Currie, Charlie Hussey, Bob Ashworth (CO), Val Hawes (SObs), 'Tubby' Leonard (SP), Nick Taylor, Ken Readings, Joe Jones, Doug Fawcett, Peter Green and George White. In the front row, Jem Tetley is third from the left, next to the mascot. The 'Flying Tels', not featured here, were Tels or Tel (A)s L. Attwood, Fields, Dixon, Hussey, M. J. Rick, Watson, Bennett, W. M. McKenzie and R. J. Noyes. The mascot is a chinthe, 'liberated' from No 257 Squadron RAF when 825 was visiting Wattisham.

Opposite, lower: 825 Squadron's Gannets in anchor formation.

Party Pieces *Lieutenant-Commander Patrick Rogers*

My time in Gannets was fairly brief as no sooner had I joined 825 Squadron in 1957 than the Defence Review of the time decided that all the Gannets were to go. Nevertheless, in 1957 the RN was keen to show off its newest aircraft in squadron service, the Sea Hawk and the Gannet, so, a combined sequence was put together for the Farnborough Air Show—a solo Sea Hawk, a Sea Hawk formation aerobatic team, and four Gannets in diamond formation. The Gannet, of course, not being in the least aerobatic, was incapable of doing anything spectacular: its normal 'party piece' was to demonstrate its versatility at shutting down and re-starting an engine.

Because it was Farnborough, some bright spark suggested that it would be more impressive if the start-and-stop manœuvres were demonstrated by a formation of four aircraft. The process of starting and stopping an engine results in some quite marked changes in an aircraft's speed, so each step in the cockpit drill, particularly the moment of light-up, would have to be perfectly sychronised if we were to avoid an untidy wobble in the formation. Things did

COURTESY PATRICK ROGERS

COURTESY PATRICK ROGERS

COURTESY PATRICK ROGERS

Right, upper: 825 Squadron air crew, photographed at Hal Far in 1958. Seventh from the left is Don Currie, and then, in order, are David Husband, Doug Fawcett, Charlie Hussey, Pat Symonds, Peter Green, Val Hawes (SObs), John Baillie, Bob Ashworth (CO), John Taylor, Tubby Leonard (SP), Malcolm Carver, Nick Taylor, Pat Rogers, Julian Hattersley (USN), Joe James, Jem Tetley, Ken Reedings, Keith Sumner and (behind the four Flying Tels on the right) Pete De Souza.

COURTESY PATRICK ROGERS

become a bit unstuck during a rehearsal one day when the three formating aircraft suddenly found themselves overtaking the leader. This was not too dramatic for the wingmen, but George White, who was number four in the box, found himself getting a very intimate view of the underside of the leader's Gannet as he swept past him. George himself explains:

'The procedure was to advance the throttle of the engine to be retained, close the throttle of the engine to be stopped, put the HP cock down to the "feather and brake" (bottom) position which shut off the fuel and started the feathering process and, finally, press the relight button when the revs had dropped to 3,000. As a "show-stopper" at Farnborough, we were going to do this while flying in close formation, our wings overlapping by about six feet and the one in the box with his prop about six feet behind the leader's hook.

'Our Senior P, Tubby Leonard, was leading our four. Doug Fawcett was number two, Pat Rogers was number three on the right and I was in the box. At the order "Stand by to stop port engine . . . stop port engine . . . now!", we all began the procedure. Unfortunately, Tubby's HP cock did not go beyond the central "off"position, with the result that his prop went fully fine instead of feathering and therefore acted as a very efficient air brake. Pat and Doug raised their wings in response and safely passed the leader; my reaction was smartly to close the going throttle, but as that was insufficient I pushed the nose forward and watched Tubby go safely back—as I thought—over my head. However, it engendered the comment from my telegraphist facing

COURTESY BRIAN LOWE

Right: XA457 of the Squadron in the standard scheme of the day. The aircraft has unoccupied rocket rails beneath the wing.
Below: 'Gosh, sir, that was a bit close!'—but in fact it was rather more than that, as shown by the serrated tip of XA458's rudder after its brush with the propellers of the Senior Pilot's Gannet XG783.

COURTESY BRIAN GRINDLEY

COURTESY GEORGE WHITE

rearwards in the rear cockpit , "Gosh, sir! That was a bit close!", to which I replied, "Missed me by at least twelve feet at this end!" We duly got ourselves sorted out and did not discover how close things had been until after landing at the end of the sortie.'

For the Farnborough finale the aircraft formed up as an 'anchor', and this particular manœuvre posed two challenges. First, if one was part of the 'flukes', there was some distance between one's aircraft and the next. This made it very difficult to judge the position (and any unevenness would, of course, be only too obvious from the ground). Secondly, because we made up a pretty unwieldy gaggle, the leader had rely on some very precise clockwork in order to achieve an accurate time of arrival in front of the crowd.

826 NAVAL AIR SQUADRON

Located at RNAS Lee-on-Solent and RNAS Hal Far and on board HMS *Eagle*

Commission
15/05/51–22/11/55
(A.S.1s from 17/01/55 until disbandment)

Commanding Officer
Lt-Cdr G. F. Birch (17/01/55)

Senior Pilot/Senior Observer
Not known

826 NAS was the first front-line squadron to receive Gannet A.S. Mk 1s, at Lee-on-Solent in January 1955. It was also the shortest-lived of the squadrons: it embarked in HMS *Eagle* that June merely for an exercise to prove the worth of the Gannet as an A/S aircraft and in November was promptly disbanded in order to fly helicopters.
Left: WN410 (nearest) and WN452 on *Eagle*, their spinners finished in red (forward), white and black. Each aircraft has its hold-back cable ready as it taxies towards the catapult, one end attached to the nosewheel leg and the 'deck' end held temporarily beneath the fuselage.

831 NAVAL AIR SQUADRON

Located at RNAS Culdrose and RAF Watton, with detachments to other stations and on board HM carriers as and when required

Commission
01/05/58-16/05/66 (A.S.1s 01/05/58-00/00/58, E.C.M.4s 00/02/59-00/02/61, E.C.M.6s 00/02/62-16/05/66)

Commanding Officers
Lt-Cdr W. J. Hanks, Lt-Cdr B. J. Williams (16/07/59), Lt-Cdr D. K. Blair (16/05/61), Lt-Cdr J. G. Grindle (30/05/63), Lt-Cdr M. J. Bateman (09/04/64), Lt-Cdr H. Ellis (11/06/65)

Senior Pilots/Senior Observers
Not known

A dedicated electronic countermeasures (ECM) unit, 831 Squadron initially flew Gannet A.S.1s (for pilot and crew familiarisation purposes) but these were quickly exchanged for the interim E.C.M. Mk 4s which were in turn were replaced by 'definitive' E.C.M. Mk 6s. The Squadron also flew ECM Sea Venoms. The Gannets were equipped with various active and passive electronic warfare receivers and transmitters and flights were embarked at sea in the carriers from time to time, especially during major exercises.

Below: The distinctive 831 Squadron Gannet markings comprised red finlets adorned with a yellow lightning flash, together with red (forward) and black spinners. As seen here on E.C.M. 6 XG798 (and also on page 97), in later years the 'Flook' cartoon character that had been adopted by the Squadron's Westland Wyverns back in 1956 made its appearance on the Gannet tailfins and the call-signs were changed from 300-series to 200-series, the 'last two' numerals previously carried on the ventral finlets also now being deleted. 831 NAS was based with its Royal Air Force equivalents at RAF Watton until 1966, when a combined services squadron, No 360, was formed with Canberras. Some of the Gannets were 'converted back' to Mk 4 standard for pilot training.

Bottom: A number of Gannets, on becoming redundant, were transferred to the School of Aircraft Handling at Culdrose. These two, WN464 and XA459, seen undergoing routine maintenance at that station in 1975, still wear their 831 Squadron markings.

COURTESY RICHARD L WARD

COURTESY GEOFF WAKEHAM

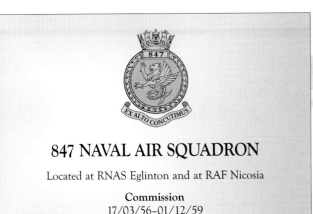

847 NAVAL AIR SQUADRON

Located at RNAS Eglinton and at RAF Nicosia

Commission
17/03/56–01/12/59
(A.S.1s until 00/06/58, A.S.4s thereafter)

Commanding Officers
Lt-Cdr W. C. Martin, Lt-Cdr W. D. Lawrence (22/03/57),
Lt-Cdr R. W. R. Hawkesworth DSC (19/05/58)

Senior Pilots/Senior Observers
Not known

Formed at RNAS Eglinton from part of 812 NAS in March 1956 for duty in Cyprus to counter gun-running to the rebels, 847 was equipped with three aircraft and these carried RNAS Hal Far ('HF') tail markings. Towards the end of the commission, at least one aircraft sported a black silhouette of the island on its finlets.
Below: Personnel of 847 Squadron on parade at Nicosia; one of their Gannets is revealed within the hangar.

COURTESY HELEN CLARKE

COURTESY HELEN CLARKE

Above: Maintenance in the Cyprus sunshine. There was much detail variation concerning the presentation of markings among the Squadron's aircraft: XA335, for example, appears always to have carried its call-sign ('086') well aft instead of on the nose, and in these photographs the aircraft lacks its Hal Far tail code although it does sport the unit crest.
Right: A.S.1 XA355 (foreground) and XA335 start their starboard engines, early 1958. Tragically, shortly after this photograph was taken XA355 crashed and all three aircrew were killed in a landing accident at Nicosia.

COURTESY HELEN CLARKE

849 NAVAL AIR SQUADRON

Located at RNAS Culdrose, RNAS Brawdy, RNAS Lossiemouth *et alibi*, and on board HM carriers, with detachments to other stations and on board HM carriers as and when required

Commission

07/07/52–15/12/78 (A.S.4s 00/09/59–00/05/66, A.E.W.3s 00/02/60–15/12/78, T.5s 00/09/61–00/01/76, C.O.D.4s 00/09/61–00/09/74)

Commanding Officers

Lt-Cdr A. G. B. Phillip (09/04/59), Lt-Cdr W. Hawley (08/12/60), Lt-Cdr J. F. McGrail (07/02/62), Lt-Cdr W. H. Barnard (17/05/63), Lt-Cdr M. J. F. Rawlinson (04/01/65), Lt-Cdr A. W. Roberts (01/08/66), Lt-Cdr B. Prideaux (07/02/68), Lt-Cdr R. M. Scott (02/05/69), Lt-Cdr J. E. Nash (04/09/70), Lt-Cdr T. Goetz (11/09/72), Lt-Cdr A. J. Light (17/04/74), Lt-Cdr G. L. J. Holman (21/08/74), Cdr T. G. Maltby (20/08/76)

Senior Pilots/Senior Observers

Lt-Cdr A. W. Roberts (Sqn SObs 1959), Lt-Cdr E. E. Eatwell (Sqn SObs), Lt P. Greenwood (SP 'A' Flt 1962), Lt P. Wilkins (SObs HQ Flt 1965)

849 Squadron has specialised in the airborne early warning (AEW) rôle since 1952, at first operating the Skyraider AEW Mk 1. After completion of 700G Flight's evaluation of the Gannet A.E.W. Mk.3 (see page 91), it accepted the assets and the Skyraiders departed. It had already established a model of an HQ squadron with up to five Flights which detached to embark in carriers. These Flights, each comprising four AEW and one COD Gannet, were not assigned to any particular carrier and were formed as required. They were identified alphabetically from A to E and each had its own distinctive aircraft markings. For training purposes the Squadron also operated Gannet A.S.4s and T.5s.

Right: XG783, a Gannet A. S. Mk 4 used by 849 Squadron 'C' Flight and HQ Flight during 1959, makes a free take-off from one of HM aircraft carriers during a training exercise.

Below: Welcome to Culdrose and the Flying Eye.

COURTESY LOU LOMHEIM

'Sir–Your Morning Tea!'

Lieutenant-Commander Lou Lomheim USN

I had just completed fours years in VAW-12 (Skyraiders) at Quonset Point, Rhode Island, when I was asked if I would go as an exchange pilot with the Royal Navy; 849 Squadron was in turn sending three RN officers to VAW-12. My wife and I hosted Lieutenant and Mrs Ron Coventry to help them get settled in America.

I checked out of VAW-12 on 26 October 1961 and flew to England, Lieutenant (jg) Ben Peper and I reporting to 849 Squadron on 4 November. I soon started ground school after being welcomed into the Royal Navy. I recall checking into the Officer's Mess and being assigned a stateroom which was quite cool (in terms of its temperature, that is) and with no way to warm it up, but the real surprise came the next morning when I heard a woman's voice in my stateroom: 'Sir–I have your morning tea!' No one had briefed me on this custom!

The ground school was short and very much to the point. I was finding some of the terminology to be different than I was used to hearing–aluminium, centrifugal, etc.–but within a short time, on 27 November, Lieutenant White was giving me three indoctrination flights in the Gannet T.5 and soloing me two days later. I was really impressed with how easy it was to hold heading at full power. I had been flying the AD5W Skyraider with the 2,800hp R3350 engine, which needed a lot of rudder for take-offs and carrier landings, especially when on the back side of the power curve. The real secret for the Skyraider was being trimmed out for the flight profile you were in at any given time. I found the Gannet really neat to fly, with little rudder needed to keep it straight for take-offs on both land and ship.

I recall one incident that occurred in flight from Culdrose. I do not remember the names of the senior RN Observer and of the RN student, but I was looking out on the left wing and noticed that the visual locking device had come out of the wing. I mentioned this to the crew and great concern was expressed by them to me. I very quickly was given vectors back to Culdrose and I began a very gradual turn to take us home. The maintenance people did a complete check of the system but, as I recall, could not figure out what was causing the problem. It was disconcerting for us in the aircraft because it meant that the lock of the lock, so to speak, had failed!

I was assigned to 'A' Flight in June 1962 and we deployed to HMS *Centaur*, taking part in the NATO exercise 'Fairwind VII' in the North Atlantic. On its completion, *Centaur* went to her home port of Devonport for a few weeks and 'A' Flight returned to Culdrose for a stand-down before deploying to the Mediterranean area. The ship and air wing left for the Med in late July and took part in NATO exercise 'Riptide II'. We took part in a cross-deck operation with the USS *Enterprise* and USS *Forrestal*, and I was the

Right: 849 men: Lieutenant P. Greenwood, SP 'A' Flight (left), an unidentified lieutenant (centre) and Sub-Lieutenant V. J. Blyther, on board HMS *Centaur* with XP226.

COURTESY BRIAN LOWE

COURTESY LOU LOMHEIM

COURTESY LOU LOMHEIM

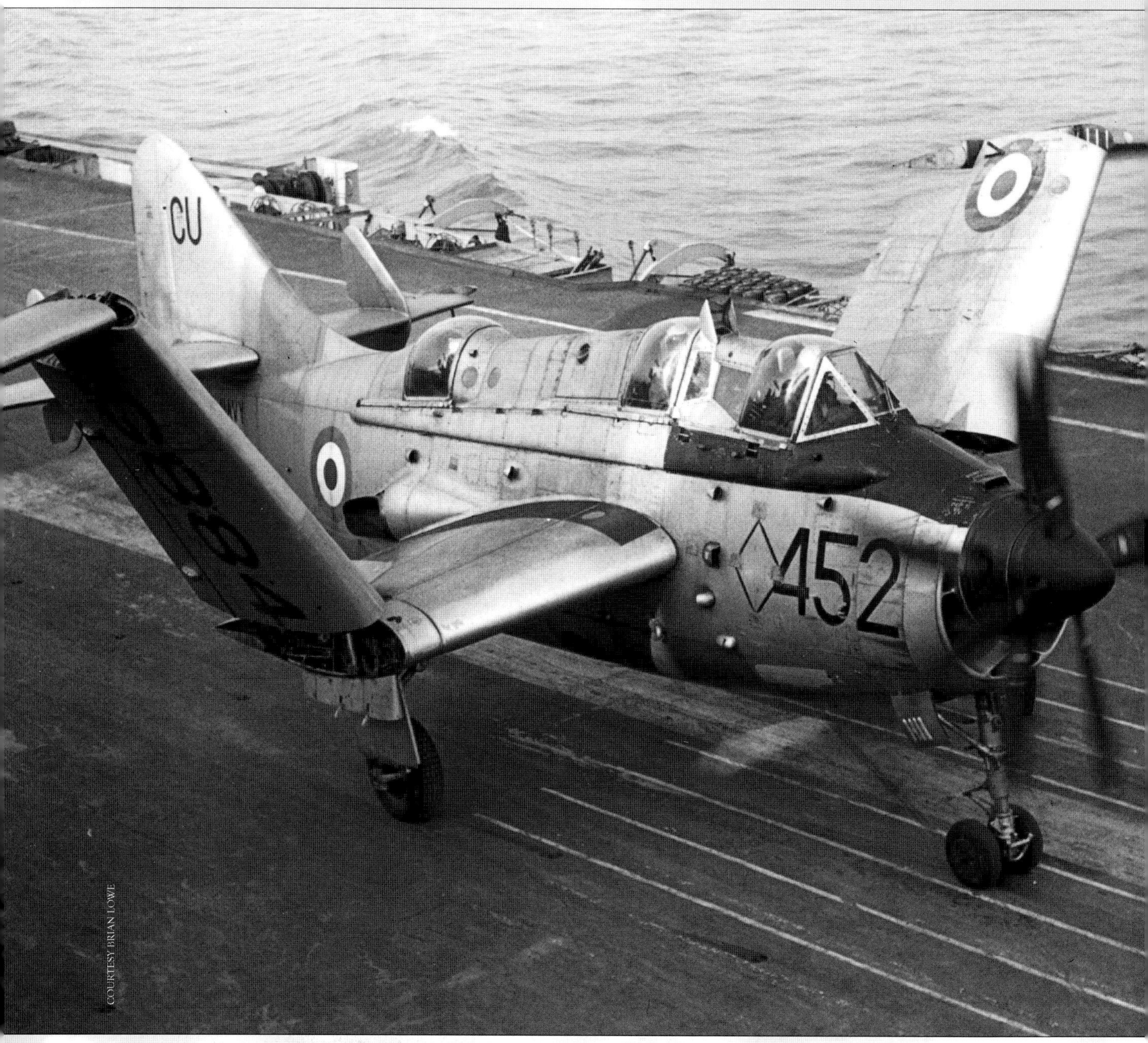

COURTESY BRIAN LOWE

pilot of the Gannet that went aboard the *Forrestal* with a US observer and one RN officer. However, the *Forrestal* people were really unhappy to see two Yanks as crew! They had gifts for the Brits and almost withheld ours! The exercise was ended with a port call at Lisbon, Portugal.

The ship proceeded into the Med with operations at the western end. We had ports of call at Marseilles, France, and Barcelona, Spain, and then it was back to Gibraltar. The ship went into dry dock for some time and we moved to RAF North Front for flight operations. 'A' Flight took time to catch up on the survival training requirements by having two helicopters take flight crews out to sea and drop them from fifty feet into the water with their flotation gear and a dinghy. The helicopter would return after several hours and make an 'at-sea rescue'. I had the feeling that this was not so much a drill as the real thing! The sea was not smooth that day, and it was with difficulty that you stayed in the dinghy!

Back at sea again, the ship's captain, Captain Sharp, was to attend a meeting with other British officers at a landing strip near El Adem, Libya. The Senior Pilot of 'A' Flight told me to report to combat control, where I met Lieutenant-Commander Rawlinson and was told that we would go to El Adem that night with the Captain. I was briefed that when we arrived I would shut down the engines and wait in the cockpit. It was a black night and my log book shows the flight was 2.8 hours long (over and back) and that it was IFR (instrument flight rules) for about half of the trip. The log also shows that the observer was Lieutenant Scott. We landed at El Adem and I, as always at night, opened the canopy to taxi so as to keep the instrument lights from reflecting on the glass. I was surprised at the hot air and fine sand that covered me right away, and, needless to say, I closed it smartly once more before finding the ground crew who parked us. The meeting was short-lived and we were soon back in the air. We made contact with the ship and were given a carrier-controlled instrument approach and landing on the ship. All went very well.

Above left: Aircrew officers of 849 Squadron in 1962. Identifiable are (seated) Sean McGrail (CO, centre), Tony Reid (SP, to his left), 'Dumbo' Newman (third from left) and Eric Taylor (third from right) and (standing) Geoff Maltby (second from left) and Ron Previ, Bill Hale USN, Peter Wilkins, Lou Lomheim USN and Ben Peper USN (fifth, sixth, seventh, eighth and tenth, respectively, from left).
Left: 849 utilised a number of Gannet trainers, including T.5 XG884 of HQ Flight shown here beginning to fold its wings having just come on board HMS *Centaur* in 1962.
Right: T. Mk 5 XG886 at RNAS Yeovilton in 1965. The radar antennas in the background duplicated the full range of equipment to be found at the time on board HM ships and provided data for the Air Direction School.
Below: XL474 comes ashore in unconventional fashion at Portsmouth, having been damaged during XP224's landing on board HMS *Hermes* on 23 October 1969.

COURTESY BRIAN LOWE

COURTESY GEOFF WAKEHAM

Observers' Odds and Ends

Lieutenant-Commander 'Paf' Grant

Ah yes—the Chart Board Hazard. Gannet AEW people will remember the plotting board available to the observer sitting in right-hand seat, and the way it slid back along a stowage rail under his radar console. The trouble was that, if it was not pushed fully home until the two securing spring clips engaged it became a positive danger—usually to the next crew to fly the aircraft. I have clear memories of a catapult shot starting with a chart board flying out of its stowage and striking me in the throat

Then there was the Low Volts Power Pack Hazard. We observers used to delay switching off the radar until the last possible moment in order to avoid the six-minute (but seemingly interminable) time-out in the event of a sudden late requirement. And how many times did procrastinators leave things late—so late, in fact, that by the time they got round to it the pilot had already throttled back and shed 400Hz before they had switched off, resulting it burn-out of the LVPP? I was just such a procrastinator on a stores run to Hal Far, from which I had to return 150 miles by dead-reckoning to *Centaur*: we could get no communications with the ship until I was well into an expanding square search—and found her 50 miles from PIM! I learnt a lesson from that!

There was, from time to time, the Unusual Tasking. During Exercise 'Swordhilt' in October 1966 I was employed on surface search/probe north of New Guinea in the area of the Bismarck Sea. A number of the skunks probed were identified as small, very low-lying coral reefs, which were uncharted and too deep for medium-range detection by ship's radar. The *Victorious* Task Group was required to make fast passage through these waters by day and night, so as a matter of urgency the Gannets were required to probe along the MLA to build up a plot of reefs, so as to produce a safe, navigable passage for the Group. I often wonder what would have happened had we not carried out this assignment.

Below: A COD (Carrier Onboard Delivery) Gannet—a converted A.S.4—of 849 'B' Flight with the tail code letter and ship's crest of HMS *Hermes*, photographed in 1966. The call sign, the single numeral '4', is carried on the forward fuselage in the usual manner.
Right, upper: 'D' Flight 849 Squadron featured dark blue and white *décor* on its Gannets, as here on XL481, assigned to *Eagle* (also seen in the photograph). The Flight's three-numeral call-signs began with a zero; the device on the fin is an adaptation of the Mahjong Red Dragon or 'Centre' symbol.
Right, lower: An 849 'A' Flight Gannet, with red and black spinners and finlets, lands on board HMS *Victorious*.

D. ROBINSON, COURTESY RICHARD L. WARD

COURTESY BRIAN LOWE

COURTESY BRIAN LOWE

Breathless and Brakelcss at Culdrose

Lieutenant Peter Randall

One fine September morning in 1964, with ground frost carpeting the grass around the squadron buildings, I, as pilot, and Ian Neale and John le Dieu as observers, walked out to an A.E.W.3 on the hardstanding and prepared for a three-hour detail off The Lizard. Before we could proceed with the main task, however, there was the small matter of a taxi test to perform, as the aircraft had been the subject of a brake pad change during the night. Pure routine, one would have thought, but little did we know how exciting the next hour was to be!

Pre-flight checks and engine start up were completed in the normal fashion and we moved off carefully (always carefully after work on brakes) to commence the taxi test, which merely involved a ten-minute trial to see if the brakes

COURTESY BRIAN LOWE

Above: A Mk 4 Courier Gannet carrying the dark blue overall finish standard for aircraft operating in this particular rôle. The aircraft is assigned to 'B' Flight on board HMS *Ark Royal*, 1970, and has the yellow and black ('bee'-related) spinner and finlet markings of the unit together with a stylised 'B' within the diamond formed by the crew access footholds.

Right: 849 'C' Flight aircraft were characterised by black and white markings, and the 'ownership' of this A.E.W.3, XP224, is further emphasised by the individual letter beneath the front cockpit. This photograph was taken on the occasion of the Fleet Air Arm's fiftieth anniversary celebrations at RNAS Yeovilton in May 1964.

worked correctly. This they did initially, but after about three minutes there was suddenly no response from the foot brakes located on the rudder pedals. Now, in most aircraft fitted with a nose wheel this would not have been too problematic as the nose wheel is used to steer—but not in the Gannet! The Gannet has a fixed nose wheel and steering is achieved by locking the wheel briefly on the side towards which the aircraft is to be turned by means of pressure on the appropriate foot brake. Thus it follows in the Gannet—no brakes equals no steering! As if that were not enough, the aircraft was actually pointing slightly downhill at the time; and, to my horror , it was beginning to accelerate. In desperation I grabbed hold of the parking brake and pulled it fully 'on', but the acceleration continued.

The awful truth now dawned that there was no way of stopping this machine in its headlong rush down an ever steepening incline, and, to make matters worse, the ground was hard, for by now we were on the grass which was mown short and covered in frost. A great flurry of arms and legs then ensued in the cockpit as I shut down the engines. This was positively the last card I could play, but it was to no avail as the speed continued to build up. We sailed past the engineers' office with the starboard wing very close to the windows, which were now filled with a row of little white faces all looking up at me. Bizarrely, I had an overwhelming urge to give them a cheery wave, but I was far too busy!

Left: The flight line at Culdrose—downhill in all directions.

Another building hove in sight and this time it was dead ahead. It was the ratings' crew room, and I realised that our journey was about to end. I could see the off-duty watch playing cards around the table with a chap standing up, dealing; he looked idly in my direction and then carried on with his task. We were by this time very close, and suddenly he understood the imminent calamity and the place erupted. They could not all get out of the door, and so some hid behind clothing lockers, others jumped out of windows, and I actually saw a grown man wriggle out of a fanlight window.

The effect was very Laurel and Hardy and now affords me a grin every time I think of it, but during the event it was difficult to raise a laugh. When the crunch came it really wasn't too bad, but it resulted in a severely shock-loaded Double Mamba and a crumpled starboard wing tip. Importantly, no one was hurt. Later it was realised that it was very fortunate that we had hit that building, because the next stop would have been a drop of about ten feet on to the main road from Helston to The Lizard. Just imagine the surprise of the motorists!

Subsequently, it was discovered that the problem had been caused by a faulty batch of brake pads that burned out instantaneously, but there was to be one more irony. When the aircraft hit the crew room, one propeller was still revolving, and it sliced through the roof and ended up less than two inches from a 440-volt cable. Had it connected, the result would have sharpened us up no end.

RICHARD L. WARD

Crazy Brits

Commander Colin Watkins

Back in 1975, when HMS *Ark Royal* was operating with the USS *Independence* on an exercise off the East Coast of the United States, the American E-2B Hawkeye fleet was grounded because of a problem and the Royal Navy offered two Gannets to transfer to 'Indy' to fill the AEW slots. The Senior Pilot, Ken Patrick, experienced 'looker' Tom McGhee and a younger 'looker'—me—were sent to 'Indy' for a recce. The landing was good and the Americans were impressed with Ken's ability to stay on the meatball's bore-sight. All was filmed, of course, and we saw it several times.

After we had met the Admiral, Captain and 'Wings' ('CAG Boss', or something like that) and been given our leather jackets, we separated to complete our recce tasks, Ken to talk about flying and maintenance, Tom on ops and me on domestics, accommodation, eating and, importantly, drinking (big problem!) However, my difficulties were subsumed by the biggest one—how to take-off. We were carrying a new strop, but, in the planning by those who no longer use the ACRB (Air Crew Refreshment Bar), one tiny thing had been overlooked: the US Navy did not now launch aeroplanes using strops! They used nose-wheel attachments, and we knew that, even if one could be fitted to the Gannet, all that would be launched would be the nose-wheel. I recall lots of high level R/T between the Senior Pilot and 'Ark', the outcome being that we would do a free take-off.

Ken was an experienced COD pilot but I think it was going to be his first free take-off in a Mk 3. However, as he would say, '*Pas de problème!*' We were spotted by the round-down facing along the angle, and 'Indy' wound up to launch speed. News had got around the ship that some 'crazy Brits' were about to perform something unusual, and 'goofers' was moderately full. The hand came down and off we went, but unfortunately we sheered off to starboard. (Remember—the Gannet did not have a steerable nose wheel, just differential braking on the main wheels.) Ken managed to stop safely, and we turned round with difficulty and taxied back down the deck. By now the ship was at full speed into wind and there was a gale blowing us along. When we turned to line up, the inside wheel skidded on the greasy deck and only fast action by an American football-player-sized 'chockhead' with a deck strop prevented us sliding over the stern! By now the word had got around that 'the Brits' were providing great entertainment with the possibility of self-sacrifice, 'goofers' was crowded and bets were being taken. Disappointingly for the crowd, the take-off was text-book, although in the back I recall being rather concerned that the ASI did not start to register until we were clear of the deck.

Back in 'Ark', the idea of cross-decking for the rest of the exercise was quietly shelved and 849B Flight, just like 809 (Buccaneers) and 892 (Phantoms), could enjoy a twelve-hour stand-off every day!

Below: XL482, assigned to 'B' Flight on board *Ark Royal* at the time of Commander Watkins' adventures on board the USS *Independence*.

COURTESY PHILIP JARRETT

COURTESY PHILIP JARRETT

Above: The flight-deck routine: 'A' Flight's XL474, with smart trim on its drop tanks, is steered by handlers towards its parking slot on board *Hermes*, 1969. This was the aircraft involved in the accident mentioned on page 135.

Below: 'A' Flight, its aircraft in pristine condition, prepares to start engines at Brawdy in 1968; nearest is XL451. A lowered arrester hook was often evident on a parked aircraft—usually because of hydraulic seepage.

COURTESY BRIAN LOWE

Reflections

Commander Michael J. Doust

I have fond memories of the Gannet, although I had few hours actually piloting the aircraft. My first experience of flying it was at RNAS Ford, where I had been appointed to 764 Squadron for the Wyvern conversion course. The Wyvern was, like the Gannet, turboprop-powered with a contra-rotating propeller unit, although of course it had only one engine and not two. Even so, it was considered a good idea that all Wyvern conversion pilots take a demonstration flight in the Gannet to be shown how a turbo-prop jet engine handled, both on the ground and in the air. I drove over to 700 Squadron on the western side of Ford, and on 2 July 1955 I was flown in a Gannet A. S. Mk 1 by Lieutenant-Commander Stan Farquhar, the Squadron's Senior Pilot. He gave me a very pleasant demo-flight, and I landed with the feeling that I had some idea how a turbo-prop aircraft might handle. The flight lasted some forty minutes, but it would be another sixteen years before I flew the aircraft again.

Following appointment in 1970 to *Ark Royal* as Landing Safety Officer, I rushed around all the air bases where the carrier's Air Group squadrons were located in order to refamiliarise myself with, and where possible check out on, all the aircraft. 849 Squadron had by this time relocated to Lossiemouth, and I duly arrived at the Station in January 1971. I initially flew the Gannet T.5 dual-control trainer with Lieutenant Bainbridge, my flight instructor during my time in 849. Unfortunately, however, the Squadron's Headquarters Flight was experiencing a bad maintenance period and had only one A.E.W.3 available to fly its OFS students, so 'muggins' went to the bottom of the priority list. However, it was agreed that I could fly the T.5 as much as I liked and so, never one to look a gift horse in the mouth, I would eventually accumulate fifteen hours on type, including twelve solo. A few years later I would gain another five hours went I went through my Lieutenant-Commander (Flying) designate's courses.

A good deal of my Gannet flying at Lossiemouth was spent carrying out dummy deck landings using both

Below: An 849 Squadron 'B' Flight Gannet A.E.W.3 is manœuvred on board *Ark Royal*, on which the writer served for a period as LSO. Notice the proximity of the deck handlers to the aircraft's whirling propellers. Some of 892 Squadron's F-4K Phantoms appear in the background.

RICHARD L. WARD

engines, or with one shut down and the associated propeller feathered. On one occasion my instructor took me up to 15,000 feet to demonstrate the effect of the rear propeller disc-ing. He simulated engine failure on the rear propeller, which went instantly into fine pitch, producing what was to all intents and purposes a solid wall behind the front propeller. The aircraft's nose immediately pitched down, and with no airflow passing over the tailplane, fin and rudder, the aircraft entered a steep dive. By the time the 'failed engine' had been run back up to normal power, the aircraft had lost 8,000 feet! Apparently, 849 had recently lost an A.E.W.3 turning finals when the engine driving the rear propellers failed and the aircraft dived into the ground short of the runway, killing all its crew. I myself experienced a similar incident over northern Norway in a Wyvern when the translation bearing between the front and rear propellers failed, causing the rear propeller to go into fine pitch. Fortunately, I had an ejection seat, but I only just made it as my parachute opened as I hit the water.

I finally joined *Ark Royal* in March 1971 as the LSO, although my time on board would be short. Apart from the odd single-engine approach and deck landing, the Gannet A.E.W.3s of 849 'B' Flight carried out some of the most professional-looking deck landings in the Air Group. I left the ship in June 1971 to take command of 767 (Phantom Training) Squadron at Yeovilton, and it was while I was there that I would witness a Gannet A.E.W.3 crash on the approach to the runway during a Senior Officers' War Course air display. The aircraft had made several passes along the display runway when the pilot attempted to make a 'carrier' approach and landing in front of the Course. As the aircraft turned finals behind the Fleet Air Arm Museum, I happened to step out of my squadron office to watch the approach. The Gannet appeared from behind the Museum hangars—rather too low, in my opinion—and as it turned towards me, still sinking, I noticed that it did not have full landing flap. As the turn tightened, the sink rate increased, and the aircraft hit the tops of some trees and crashed just short of the runway. Its observer, who happened to be the CO of 849 Squadron, survived the crash apart from some bruising, but his pilot, a young lieutenant, was severely injured and died on the way to Yeovil hospital. That evening I drove over to the wardroom and met the CO of the AAIU. He took me aside and asked if I had witnessed the display and crash, and whether I had any opinions. I was quite honest and said that I thought that the pilot did not have full landing flap. 'Well, you were right,' the CO replied. 'The flap selector in the cockpit was badly corroded and the pilot only had half flap when he thought he had full flap.'

While watching an air display at Lossiemouth during the 1960s, I witnessed a another Gannet A.E.W.3 crash. A young pilot straight out of the AEW OFS training programme at RNAS Culdrose was carrying out a flight demonstration. On his second pass, single-engined along the display runway, he performed a wing-over manœuvre in front of the Control Tower, at the same time attempting to re-light the dead engine. His rear propeller disc-ed. He belly-landed in front of the spectators, and fortunately his starboard wing tip dug into the soft earth and slewed the aircraft away from the crowd. The aircraft carried on across the airfield on its nether surfaces (as seen on pages 50–51 of this book), scattering wreckage everywhere, and finally came to a halt close to the GCA Control Van, to be exited by its two-man crew, the pilot and observer, running rather fast. Unfortunately, Flag Officer Flying Training was in the Tower and had seen the accident, and he apparently had a few hard questions for the Squadron CO afterwards.

Some of the accidents involving the Gannet ended in tragic loss of life; others, looking back and with the crews known to be safe, had their funny side, most of them being attributable to pilot error. A former flying course friend of mine was carrying out circuits and landings at RNAS Eglinton on one occasion and, in order to demonstrate his 'gung-ho' qualities, he roared into the circuit like a fighter pilot, performed a hard break downwind and snapped both throttles back to idle—unfortunately, straight through the engine shut-down positions. Suddenly without power, he was obliged to make a belly landing downwind. I know of two pilots carrying out Gannet deck-landing training who went for a ducking. In the first instance, the pilot studiously carried out his external aircraft check, climbed into his cockpit, started up and spread his wings. He nodded to the FDO that he was ready to go and the FDO raised his green flag, wound him up to full power, checked that he had a 'Green' from Flyco, and lowered his flag. The pilot released the brakes and the Gannet promptly turned hard left and went over the side of the ship. The nose wheel was cocked 45 degrees to the left and neither the pilot nor the FDO, nor indeed Flyco, had noticed the fact. The aircraft should have been taxied forward slightly to straighten the nose wheel, before being wound up to full power. On the second occasion the pilot manned his aircraft at the stern of the flight deck and gave the nod that he was ready to go. The FDO wound him up to full power, checked that all was well with Flyco and lowered his flag. The aircraft accelerated along the flight deck and disappeared over the bows, straight into the briny. The pilot had failed to select take-off flap.

On a more serious note, a few years later there was a Gannet A.E.W.3 catapult accident on board *Ark Royal*, although, again, all three crew members fortunately survived to tell the tale. The aircraft had been loaded on to the bow catapult and was in the process of being tensioned and then wound up to full power. The tail holdback failed prematurely and the aircraft proceeded down the catapult under its own power. The pilot throttled back to idle and applied full brakes, but the aircraft pitched over the front end of the flight deck into the sea. The pilot and one observer managed to evacuate the aircraft as it hit the water, but the second observer went down approximately 180 feet with the Gannet. However, he managed to crawl out of the rear cockpit and ascend to the surface. He broke water, his speed so great that he rose level with the planeguard's fore deck before he fell back into the sea and was rescued. Both his eardrums were ruptured during the ascent.

I enjoyed flying the Gannet: it would do just about anything a pilot wanted it to do. Its one shortcoming lay in the dual Mamba installation. Loss of power on the engine driving the rear propeller could, on occasion, lead to disaster.

ROYAL NAVAL VOLUNTEER RESERVE

Remembered with Affection *Lieutenant (A) John Dickson RD RNVR*

I suppose it was towards the end of 1955 that we learnt that we might soon be re-equipped with Gannets. It was rumoured that the decision had been quite controversial as many of our 'Salthorse' Lordships at the Admiralty expressed doubts that part-time aviators who became Naval officers only on alternate weekends and for a couple of weeks each summer were fit to be given charge of an aeroplane that cost as much as a World War II destroyer. £250,000 each was the going rate in those days, so we were told. What seems to have been overlooked is that most of us had lots of experience, having flown in all sorts of conditions during the war. In contrast, large numbers of the next generation of air crew who made up the regular squadrons were still on a learning curve, having been trained after the war. I had noticed from my log book that I had spent very nearly 1,000 hours just flying Fairey aircraft—Swordfish, Fulmars, Barracudas and all marks of Firefly—so I was looking forward eagerly to passing an important milestone!

The Channel Air Division was the southernmost of the five RNVR air divisions, four of which comprised two squadrons and the other, the Southern Air Division, three. We operated in the anti-submarine rôle, as did the Scottish and part of the Northern Air Divisions. Our Ford-based squadrons were the only ones to receive Gannets, the others having to make do with Fireflies and Avengers.

The aircrew at Ford were in two squadrons, 1840 and 1842, and the idea was that each should operate on alternate weekends, although we joined each other for the two weeks' annual training or whenever there was a special exercise or other event requiring maximum effort. The aircraft, maintenance ratings and administrative and support staff were all 'pooled', and we were watched over by a regular staff officer and a senior Royal Navy pilot who acted as CFI. This was the general basis on which we worked, but it was a fairly loose arrangement and so, depending upon our civilian jobs, it was often possible to attend on weekdays and 'out of hours', when we could do some interesting and useful flying on various aircraft.

In January and early February 1956 three or four pilots at a time were entertained by the management and staff of the 'Rum Tum Tiddly' (i.e., Armstrong Siddeley) factory near Coventry. The groups went there in dribs and drabs, depending upon the requirements of civilian life. We were wined, dined and accommodated in a very smart hotel and spent three or four days in white coats on the factory floor and in lecture rooms discovering the workings of jet

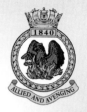

1840 and 1842 NAVAL AIR SQUADRONS

Channel Air Division, based at RNAS Ford

Believed no crest authorised for 1842 Squadron

Commission

214/04/51–10/03/57 (Gannet 1s and 2s from 00/02/56)

Commanding Officers

Cdr (A) N. H. Bovey DSC RNVR (CO CAD), Lt-Cdr (A) A. P. D. Simms RNVR (CO 1840 NAS), Lt-Cdr (A) R. A. Jameson RNVR (CO 1842 NAS)

Senior Pilots

Lt (A) R. W. Taylor RNVR (SP 1840 NAS), Lt (A) J. Dickson RNVR (SP 1842 NAS)

BRIAN LOWE

Left: One of the Channel Air Division's Gannets on the taxiway at RNAS Ford. The unit had barely begun to get to grips with its new aircraft when the decision was taken to disband all RNVR squadrons. Other RNVR divisions were scheduled to receive Gannets, but the aircraft were never issued. Opposite: A flight of three Gannet A.S.1s of the Channel Air Division, Royal Naval Volunteer Reserve, flying close to their home base, RNAS Ford, late in 1956; Arundel Castle is in the background of the photograph.

COURTESY JOHN DICKSON

engines—new to most of us—and in particular the Double Mamba turboprop that powered the Gannet. Despite travelling in wet, snowy conditions (there were no motorways in those days of course), we all agreed that the few days away from our nine-to-five office routines made an interesting and refreshing change.

I was able to arrange my annual continuous training for the last two weeks in February, when I was delighted to find two Gannet T.2 trainers, in their bright metallic finish, and two A.S.1s, in the grey and sea-green camouflage, towering above our Fireflies at the Squadron dispersal. Lieutenant-Commander Tim Mahony RN was temporarily posted to us as instructor until such time as all the RNVR pilots had satisfactorily converted to the new aircraft. I do not recall that he had any problems with us!

After a couple of hours' instruction on the T.2, spread over three trips, Tim sent me off solo on the second day. I thoroughly enjoyed myself! By the end of the month I was happily flying the A.S.1s and getting used to having two observers to care for. They coped well enough with their new back-seat 'gizmos' and were getting excellent results with the radar. Single-engine handling was a new challenge but not a difficult one, and we completed a programme of single-engine radar let-downs and GCAs among other exercises.

My first impressions of the Gannet were very favourable once I had got used to climbing aboard—access up the vertical starboard side was hardly less terrifying than climbing the north face of the Eiger, and I often wondered whether crampons and ice-pick should have been standard issue! The armchair-like seat was the most comfortable I had ever encountered, the view over the nose of the aircraft, which fell steeply away, was superb and the need to zig-zag while taxying was now redundant. Ever since my Tiger Moth days I had been taught to keep the stick well back in order to keep the tail of the aircraft down whenever the engine was running on the ground. I could forget all that now that I had a tricycle undercarriage—again, a whole new experience.

Once airborne, the Gannet flew smoothly, with no vibrations even with both engines pushing out maximum revs. The large internal weapons bay, retractable deck hook and radar 'dustbin' were all novel features, and the 'praying mantis'-like folding wing system was a huge delight. I was able to report to my dearly beloved that the Gannet was indeed a comfortable transport eminently suitable for the carriage of a married man no longer in the first flush of youth. She was quite inclined to believe me!

One Sunday morning during our familiarisation period, one of 1840's pilots was diligently practising shutting down one engine and feathering the prop when he happened to fly by the Royal Sovereign lightship. The vessel's skipper was well on the ball because, having spotted what he assumed to be an aircraft with a total engine failure, he pressed the alarm button and the entire air–sea rescue services of south-eastern England leapt into action. The lightship man must have been distinctly unpopular on a quiet Sunday as, open-mouthed, he witnessed our Gannet serenely flying off into the distance!

Over the ensuing four months we received half a dozen more A.S.1s, and a replacement for one of the T.2s arrived in October. We also took delivery of a couple of Firefly Mk 7s several weeks after we had become familiar with our Gannets. These three-seaters—these Fireflies, too, had provision for two observers—were meant as 'interims', mainly for observer training, and to bridge the gap between our two-seat Firefly A.S.6s and the new Gannets. Never mind! We enjoyed playing with them, and often used them for ferrying 'odd bods' around the country.

Bearing in mind that after the end of February we reverted to routine by flying on alternate weekends, it seems remarkable that we were sufficiently worked-up to take part in several important events during the summer months. The Home Fleet was at sea for major exercises, and we were called upon to co-operate. On another occasion we flew down to Culdrose to operate over Devonport during their Navy Day celebrations. We regularly had a submarine pretending to be a 'hostile' sailing from Portland, to act as our target during our hunter-killer exercises. Using the mirror landing aid, we practised deck landings, and although we never took our Gannets to sea—there was never a deck available—we would, I feel sure, have coped well enough. Back in 1952 we had spent a fortnight on board HMS *Triumph* with our Fireflies and had clocked up over 150 deck landings between us, all without incident. I am sure the Gannets would have proved straightforward as they were so steady and stable during the approach; there was no need continually to trim and re-trim, and with such an excellent view forward it should have been the proverbial piece of cake. Night-flying presented no difficulties either, and we practised such exercises on a couple of weekends. Most of us had experienced flying over blacked-out Britain during the war years, and so the well-lit towns and seaside resorts made it all seem like child's play.

The RNVR sailors were playing with their minesweepers one weekend, and on the Saturday afternoon I led a flight of four Gannets out over the Thames estuary with the idea of 'attacking' them. The weather was highly marginal, but we managed to stick together while the observers tried to make sense of their new radar displays. After more than half an hour with no joy, I aborted the exercise and returned to base. We needed GCA to get back in, but as we had all renewed our Green instrument ratings I envisaged no problems—and there was none. The observers were full of excuses and assumed that wooden-hulled minesweepers would have given poor radar returns. On checking with Harwich, it transpired that the 'sweepers, not liking the look of the weather, had stayed in harbour! The next day we tried again in no better weather, but this time the sailors were stung into action and must have been really impressed when four Gannets appeared out of the gloom and swept over their mastheads. Our back-seat boys decided that maybe their radar sets were not so bad after all!

At the end of June our base at Ford was open to the public at what was called a 'garden party'. During the air display we demonstrated deck-landing techniques using the mirror landing aid, but our 'party piece' involved a flight of four

Of Jetpipes and Microbursts *Lieutenant Robert Crouch RNVR*

In June 1956 I was a student at the London School of Economics and a 'weekend warrior' with 1842 Squadron, which, together with 1840 Squadron, comprised the Channel Air Division (CAD) at RNAS Ford. I was a pilot and, having just turned twenty-one, a Sub-Lieutenant (A) RNVR. The CAD was equipped with Fireflies in 1956 but in the process of converting to Mk I Gannets. My friends Gordon Williams, Jeff Clee and John Turner and I made up No 5 Gannet Conversion Course, and we had completed a three-day engine handling course at Armstrong Siddeley before commencing the flying part at Ford during our two-week summer training obligation.

My first formation flight was with Warrant Officer 'Pete' Lines and Gordon Williams. Lines had been our instructor during conversion, Williams was flying Number Two in the formation and I was flying Number Three. I had only completed a few hours in the Gannet (number '863', my log book tells me) and so, essentially, I was still in the 'familiarisation' phase.

We rolled on to the runway and began to accelerate towards the east (and Littlehampton). As we picked up speed, I detected an acrid smell in the cockpit. I glanced down at the fire warning lights quickly, but they were both black. In retrospect I should have aborted the take-off anyway because the acrid smell was getting worse, but you know how it is: I did not want to make myself look like a fool—especially since, every time I glanced, the fire warning lights remained black.

We rotated and were soon airborne. By now the stench was almost overwhelming. I was just about to tell Lines that I thought something was wrong and that I was returning to base, when Williams announced that a generator failure warning light had come on in his aircraft. Lines and Williams started discussing that problem. Meanwhile, my situation was deteriorating rapidly. I could actually see smoke in the cockpit now and my eyes were watering. Clearly, something was burning, whatever the fire warning lights indicated (which was nothing).

I broke to starboard and declared an emergency to Ford, requesting a straight-in, downwind landing because of fire (screw the fire warning lights, which were still black!). I was too low to bail out—and would not have, even if I could, because the Gannet might have wiped out a good half of

Right: No 5 Gannet Conversion Course: (left ro right) Gordon Williams, Jeff Clee, John Turner and Robert Crouch. In the immediate postwar years a very few young men were permitted to train as naval aircrew as part of their National Service, a requirement being that they continue in the Reserves, as pilots or observers, for four years thereafter.

Gannets lined up like guardsmen, with wings folded, facing the crowds. On the leaders signal four Double Mambas sprang into life amidst puffs of blue smoke. Having settled down with the other engines turning and burning, we executed a smart turn to port and taxied out at close intervals. At a given point just short of the threshold, we spread our wings and took off in succession. When the four aircraft had split up, the leader flashed past the crowd going downwind and downhill with both engines at maximum revs. Meanwhile Number Two staggered back into wind in deck-landing mode with wheels, flaps and hook extended. Number Three (me) banked in front of the upturned faces with the capacious weapons bay open and displaying racks of dummy ordnance and with the radome extended. Number Four's task was to shut down one engine and hope that the prop windmilled to a stop in front of the spectators. At the close of the display, having re-formed and carried out a stream landing, we taxied back and parked wing tip to wing tip with military precision. On the leader's signal the wings were folded and the engines shut down in unison.

Duty weekends seldom passed without interest, and my log book records Army co-operation exercises, shipping reconnaissance in the Channel, overland and sea navigation exercises, sonobuoy-laying and mutual instrument flying in the T.2s and in the pair of Sea Balliol T.21s that we also had on station. On Sunday 16 December 1956, after a two-hour anti-submarine patrol exercise in Gannet A.S.1 WN463 (coded '857'/'FD'), I taxied in and helped my two observers out of the back seats with all their paraphernalia. It transpired that this was my last flight in a Royal Navy aeroplane. During the Christmas leave period we received a 'Don't call us—we'll call you' signal from Their Lordships advising us that the RNVR squadrons were being disbanded and that there would be no more flying. My crew on that last trip were Maurice Humphreys, who had been my regular observer for the past five years, and Denis Rice, whom I had first met at the end of the war when he had joined our ship in Sydney. Both recalled that our last flight together had been problem-free and that the landing had been especially smooth!

We returned to Ford on a couple of occasions, once to hand in all our flying gear and again for a farewell parade attended by Admiral Commanding Reserves. It would be an understatement to say that our hearts were not in it: all our aeroplanes had been redistributed or safely tucked away. On 10 March 1957 the eleven RNVR air squadrons and twenty-one Royal Auxiliary Air Force squadrons were officially disbanded, and, at the stroke of a pen, more than 500 highly experienced aircrew and a greater number of support personnel were made redundant. However, I doubt whether we would have continued flying Gannets in the anti-submarine rôle for much longer than we did. To protect convoys, a good-sized flight deck would have needed to be part of the fleet, and, as we now know, the days of the RN's conventional carriers were numbered. I doubt whether many of us would have relished being retrained as helicopter pilots, even if the opportunity had been offered.

Today, as an old man, I look with affection at the Gannets on display in the museums at Duxford and Yeovilton—although my first thoughts are, 'How on earth did I ever manage to climb aboard?' and 'What would it have been like on a wind- and rain-swept flight deck?'

COURTESY ROBERT CROUCH

COURTESY ROBERT CROUCH

COURTESY ROBERT CROUCH

Above: XA352/'856' was the Gannet in which Robert Crouch had a 'near thing' when, on 13 June 1956, its port jetpipe came adrift; these views of the aircraft show the extent of the problem. It is easy to imagine how much worse the consequences might have been for all concerned.

Littlehampton. The acrid white smoke was now choking me, so I wound back the canopy as I lined up for the downwind landing. The wind was calm, so this was no big deal.

As soon as I touched down, I stood on the brakes and simultaneously began to shut down both engines. As I slowed, thick white smoke engulfed me even though the canopy was wide open. I was coughing and choking, and as the aircraft shuddered to a halt I pulled on the emergency brake, hit both harness and 'chute releases, and then slithered over the side harry quickers. It's a big drop from the cockpit of a Gannet. The blood and fire wagons were right there, so I hobbled towards them, fearing that the Gannet might blow at any second. A plume of white smoke was now rising twenty feet into the air.

At the inquiry, it turned out that the port jetpipe had been improperly installed. Instead of being 'u'-clamped to a one-inch flange at the end of the engine nacelle, the clamp had been attached to the one-eighth-of-an-inch-wide rim surrounding the nacelle flange. The rim had held for five flying hours (the aircraft's servicing record showed) before giving way on my flight.

When it gave way on my take-off, the jet-pipe slipped aft about eighteen inches before it hit an emergency retaining bolt. As a result, there was an eighteen-inch gap between the engine fairing and the jetpipe. Consequently, the hot exhaust gases were venting not to the outside but to the interior of the fuselage, where all sorts of things had begun to burn or melt.

Why were the fire-warning lights not activated? The answer is that the Gannet's fire sensors surrounded the engine fairings (which were not on fire) but there were no fire sensors within the fuselage (which *was* on fire). The fitter who had negligently misconnected the jetpipe to the engine was reprimanded.

* * *

It was a Sunday afternoon at the end of August 1956. I was on a solo milk-run from Ford to RNAS Culdrose and back. I took off from Culdrose to return to Ford at about 1500 hours. The air was humid and the Met people at Culdrose had mentioned the possibility of thunderstorms. Sure enough, as I headed up the Channel the cumulus clouds were evolving into cumulo-nimbus and the sky was darkening rapidly. I could see lightning in the distance. I shopped around for potential diversionary fields, but they were all reporting the same conditions. So, on the principle 'better the devil you know than the devil you don't', I pressed on towards Ford. I held a white card instrument rating and had actual instrument time in excess of thirty hours, so I was comfortable on the clocks. Nonetheless, I knew well enough that I should stay clear of thunderstorms if I possibly could.

My track was taking me across the southern part of the Isle of Wight, and by the time I was abreast Weymouth there were thunderstorms over the island and as far across the Channel as the eye could see. The tops were well above my service ceiling, so there was no question of going over them—it was either through them or under them. I decided on the latter. The cloud base was about two thousand feet and I was doing about two hundred knots. Normally, when approaching Ford on this track, I turned on the second engine after clearing the island, but this time I decided to turn it on before reaching it. I reasoned that I did not want to be dealing with a re-start in heavy turbulence.

As I went underneath the thunderstorm there was torrential rain but, to my surprise, very little turbulence. Then all hell broke loose. My nose shot sixty degrees up into the air and, even though I had been doing two hundred knots the moment beforehand, the airspeed indicator dropped off the scale and the rate of climb indicator hit the bottom stop. My instincts told me that the plane was not flying but instead dropping like a rock. I slammed the stick forward and firewalled both throttles. The plane did not respond. It was like being on a frictionless water-slide.

One thing can be said about the Gannet: the pilot had a splendid view. I could see with perfect clarity the Channel rushing up to grab me—and I was sure it was going to do just that. I even remember uttering the pilot's last prayer, 'Oh sh**!' I was only feet from the water when the plane 'bit' into the air and started rocketing skyward because it was suddenly at two hundred knots again and at full power in a huge nose-up attitude.

Before the nose came down, I had shot into the very thunderstorm I had been trying to avoid. 'Keep the wings level! . . .Keep the wings level! . . .' I kept repeating to myself as I tried to maintain control. There was no question of maintaining altitude, however: the rate-of-climb indicator was ricocheting from stop to stop as the plane went up and down like a whore's drawers on boat-race night. I got the nose level and eased off the power to try to get down out of the storm. After a few minutes of turbulent descent I caught a glimpse of the Channel and Selsey Bill and I uttered the biggest sigh of relief known to man.

I ran the scud towards Ford, who gave me a straight in. When I parked the plane, I was shaking like a leaf. Don't let anyone tell you we're not descended from fishes—my gills were fluttering physically. And I was ashen white. I wanted to de-brief, but everyone had headed home because of the weather and so I, too, made for London. When my mother opened the door she looked at me and said, 'What happened to you, Robert? You look like a blonde in a green dress!'

With the benefit of hindsight, we know exactly what happened: I had gone through a microburst. But this was 1956, and the Oxford English Dictionary records that the first use of the term 'microburst' in a meteorological context appeared in 1981.

I had emigrated to the United States in the wake of the Sandys axe to the Reserves in 1957. I have been Professor of Economics at the University of California, Santa Barbara, for the past forty years (but have also continued to potter around the sky as a member of a Cessna 172 partnership). I have always subscribed to the National Transportation Board's accident reports and, as a result, have been able, over time, to piece together what had happened to me.

The first analogy with my predicament was Eastern Airlines Flight 66 on 24 June 1975 at JFK, which crashed while landing when thunderstorms were in the vicinity, and there are references to seven other similar fatal crashes between 1982 and 2007. As I read the details of each incident when they occurred, I became more and more convinced that I, too, had been in a microburst back in 1956. I believe I survived the experience for three reasons. First, I had both engines turned on. Normally, one would only wind up the second engine after clearing the Isle of Wight, but, as I said, I turned it on early to keep my work load at a minimum in case things turned ugly. Secondly, I was flying at a much greater altitude than those aircraft that had not survived when the microburst hit. Thirdly, I had firewalled both throttles and the stick the second I recognised that plane was not actually flying. Had I not reacted instantaneously, I do not think I would have made it. I was only feet from the 'oggin when my ugly old Gannet 'bit' into the air again—bless her beautiful heart!

Below: A formal photograph of the personnel of 1842 Squadron taken in front of the Wardroom at Ford at the time of the Farewell Parade in 1957: (seated, left to right) Lieutenant-Commander Jack Stewart (O), Lieutenant John Dickson (SP), Commander N. H. ('Crash') Bovey DSC (CO CAD), Vice-Admiral Geoffrey Thistleton-Smith (Admiral Commanding Reserves), Lieutenant-Commander Ralph Jameson (CO), Lieutenant R. H. ('Red') Redman (SObs), Lieutenant-Commander Ted Margetts; (second row) Lieutenants John Elliott and Adrian Risso-Gill (O), Sub-Lieutenants Freddie Walsh, John Phillips, Ralph Hayward and Bill Box (P), Lieutenant Jeff Clee (P), Lieutenant Maurice Humphries (O); (back row) Sub-Lieutenant Robert Crouch (P), Midshipman Tim Whitaker (P), Sub-Lieutenants Nigel Sitwell (P) and John Kidd and Lieutenants Tom Miller-Jones, Paddy Prior (P) and Vic Spelman (O).

COURTESY ROBERT CROUCH

OTHER GANNET UNITS

Unit	Remarks
Aeroplane and Armament Experimental Establishment	At Boscombe Down.
Royal Aircraft Establishment	At Farnborough and Bedford.
Royal Radar Establishment	At Pershore.
Torpedo Trials Unit	At Culdrose.
Empire Test Pilots' School	At Farnborough.
Maintenance Test Pilots' School	At Abbotsinch.
Naval Aircraft Support Units	At Brawdy, Culdrose, Lossiemouth and Hal Far and at RAF Changi.
Receipt and Dispatch Unit	At Anthorn.
Station Flights	Various RN air stations.
COD Flight/Ships' Flights	On board fleet carriers *Ark Royal*, *Eagle*, *Hermes*, *Victorious*.
School of Aircraft Handling	At Culdrose.
Aircraft Holding Units	At Ford, Abbotsinch, Culdrose and Lossiemouth.

COURTESY PHILIP JARRETT

COURTESY PHILIP JARRETT

RICHARD L. WARD

Left, upper: Gannet XJ440—the aerodynamic prototype for the A.E.W. Mk 3—first flew on 20 August 1958. It proved the Double Mamba 102 in the new airframe but had no radar installed, and it featured a non-standard tail 'bumper' beneath the rear fuselage. Several Gannets were used by 'C' Squadron A&AEE at Boscombe Down for aircraft, weapons and systems development, and XJ440 served briefly in this programme.
Left, lower: A.E.W. Mk 3 XL500 in 1984 when the aircraft was involved in trials being carried out by Dowty-Rotol in connection with studies into propeller noise. The boom along the port fuselage carries sensitive acoustics equipment.
Above: T.2 XG873 on ETPS charge in September 1963 and awaiting transfer to the Aircraft Holding Unit at Abbostsinch.
Right: WN429 (coded '24') during its brief service with the ETPS at Farnborough in 1955; see page 78 for another view of this Gannet. Later that year the aircraft was transferred to 737 Squadron.

COURTESY PHILIP JARRETT

RICHARD L. WARD

Left, upper: XA508/'627' was the first Gannet T.2 to be delivered to the Royal Navy. It is seen here, semi-derelict (but still, just about, in the markings of its original operator, 737 Squadron) at Yeovilton in 1977. Repainted, it currently resides at the Midland Air Museum on loan from the FAA Museum. It is thought to be the only T.2 extant.
Left, lower: WN346 at Lee-on-Solent in August 1963, by this time a non-flying airframe. Although this A.S.1 bears the Guinness harp of 815 Squadron, the aircraft appears never to have served with that unit and the finlets are probably replacements substituted purely for decorative purposes.
Below: Victim of the 'Sandys axe' and derelict at Abbotsinch dump—WN360, late of 796 Squadron, in 1960.

RICHARD L. WARD

RICHARD L. WARD